D0253154

All Terrain Biking

Skills and techniques for mountain bikers

"Get out there and ride!"

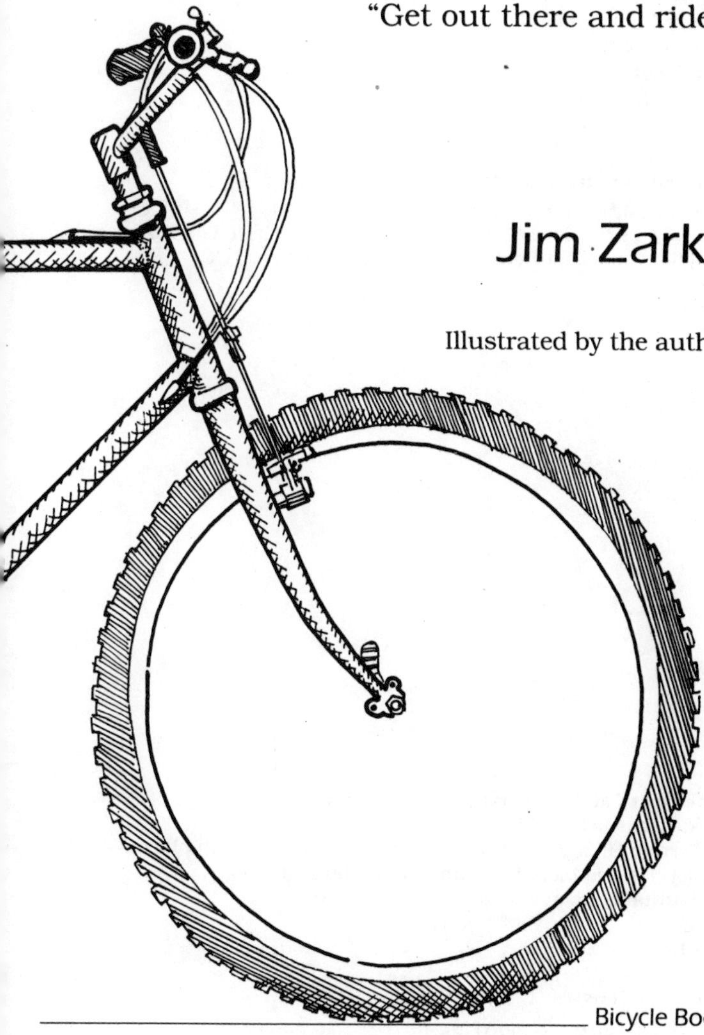

Jim Zarka

Illustrated by the author

Bicycle Books

First printing 1991
Second printing, revised, 1992

Printed in the United States of America

Published by:
Bicycle Books, Inc.
PO Box 2038
Mill Valley CA 94941

Distributed to the book trade by:

USA: National Book Network, Lanham, MD
UK: Chris Lloyd Sales and Marketing Services, Poole, Dorset
Canada: Raincoast Book Distribution, Vancouver, BC

Publisher's Cataloging in Publication Data:
Zarka, James J., 1955—
All Terrain Biking, Skills and techniques for mountain bikers.
1. Bicycles and bicycling, handbooks and manuals.
2. Mountains, recreational use.
I Title.
II Author.

Library of Congress Catalog Card No. 91-70409

Paperback ISBN 0-933201-38-9

Acknowledgements

Whatever the copyright page says, this book is not the work of a single individual: many others have provided very substantial contributions. In particular, I should thank Andy Kline, who is largely responsible for the chapters on preparedness skills, Linda Crockett and Monica Woolsey, who essentially wrote the chapters on kinesiology and nutrition, respectively, maintenance guru Eric Paul for the information contained in the chapter on maintenance, and Andria Bronsten for editing our work.

Thanks also go to the many people who have provided helpful advice and information. Here I should mention the City of Boulder Mountain Park rangers, Cameron Gloss, Paul Kuhn, Stacy Smith, Virginie Malteste, Joe Vigil, Doug Emerson and Tony Dalessandro, as well as University Bicycles, Maurice (Mo) Bray, and Dave Felkley of Manufacturer's Sports Outlet in Boulder, Colorado.

About the Author

Jim Zarka is a landscape architect and illustrator living in mountain biking paradise Boulder, Colorado. He holds a Bachelor's degree in Landscape Architecture from Michigan State University and has variously worked as a park designer, landscape architect and architectural illustrator since graduation in 1979. He was one of a team who wrote the *First Michigan Solar Energy Catalog* for the Michigan State Department of Energy. He has also worked as a landscape architect on 15 miles of bicycle trails along the South Platte River, Boulder Creek and the Yampa River in Colorado.

He has been riding mountain bikes hard and eagerly since 1982, after he discovered that the best way to defend his body from entropy was to take up an active sport that took him into nature. He met a friend who had just bought a mountain bike, tried it out for a spin around the block, and was sold on the sport for good. He is particularly keen to see the mountain bike used as a gentle means of access to nature, never to subdue or offend it. He has written environmental responsibility in his banner and shows that environmentally responsible mountain bike riding can be fun.

The motto of this book is *"Get Out There and Ride!"* That is the most important thing you will need to do to understand your mountain bike. Practice will allow you to become a competent cyclist. By reading sections of this manual, you will learn to become a better, and more prepared, mountain biker.

Some of the information presented you'll be able to use immediately, others will seem most relevant under specific circumstances. Skim through the book, and highlight important sections so you can come back to them. Read sections of the book as they appeal to you; by reading a chapter or two every so often, you will get more from the book. Whenever you can, practice the techniques described while riding. Then re-read the pertinent sections. That is the best way to translate theory into reality.

There are a lot of techniques that will take a good understanding of your bike and your sense of balance. Be patient: they will reveal themselves as your ability increases. Ride on!

Table of Contents

Chapter 1
_____ Respect

Hey: Stop, look, listen!

You must have respect. It is the key word in mountain biking. It encompasses every aspect of the sport. It is you, your bike and the environment. Your level of responsibility on the bicycle directly influences your own life as well as the lives of people, animals and plants surrounding you.

Self Respect

First, respect yourself. Wear proper clothing to protect you from the elements. You may want additional padding for tough, technical rides. Wear comfortable non-restrictive clothing that is not so loose that it will get snagged on the bike or other objects. Wear a helmet and riding gloves. Riding gloves will cushion and protect your hands from vibration and abrasion. If you do fall, the best way is to land either on your feet or on your feet and hands. When falling on smooth soft surfaces, roll with the fall. Take along clothing that will protect you from the range of weather conditions you may encounter during the ride.

Helmets

There are two forms of helmet approvals prevalent in the United States: ANSI (American National Standard Institute) and Snell Memorial Foundation. The helmet approval sticker assures that the helmet has met certain minimum criteria as specified by the relevant institute. Don't buy a helmet unless you are sure it meets those safety standards. Compare specifications for non-stickered helmets with helmets carrying one of the previously discussed stickers.

Until recently, there were just two basic types of helmets, hard shell and soft shell. The hard shell helmet is more durable in its protection. More recently, 'micro shell' helmets were introduced, which have a thin armor shield on the helmet's exterior surface. A bonus of this technology is that these helmets often weigh no more than a soft shell helmet. Soft shell helmets are made of a thick lightweight material, typically polystyrene. This material provides excellent impact protection. A helmet's hard outer surface helps prevent sharp objects from penetrating. Carefully read the helmet manufacturer's instructions for adjusting it to your head: it should fit snugly.

A helmet should be replaced after an accident involving its use. If the helmet made impact with your head in it, the liner may be crushed, making the helmet ineffective in a subsequent accident. Even a hard shell helmet may well be damaged and should be replaced, even if no damage is outwardly visible.

Climate Awareness

Imagine you are stranded by weather conditions, injury or mechanical problems. If not prepared for this possibility by taking clothing and supplies that would allow you to survive potential climate changes, you could lose your life. Realize it freezes and snows in mountainous regions earlier and later in the year than at lower altitudes. Year-round, hypothermia is a potential killer. Most cases of hypothermia occur on humid days with the temperature in the mid-sixties Farenheit (17—20°C). Especially above the tree line, electric storms can appear quickly and may be deadly. Respect the concept that death by heat stroke and dehydration in an arid environment is a real possibility, so carry plenty of water under those circumstances. Know preparedness and survival techniques if you ride in seldom traveled areas. Know how to get back by using respectful trail marking methods.

Skill Level

Ride with respect for your own skill level. Push the en-

Before the black limousine ...

velope towards more difficult and technical moves in an incremental way. Move slowly when practicing a new technique. Think about the dynamics between you, the bike and the ground. The secret structure of a skill will become clear with practice (persistence and time). The more you do anything, the better you become at it. Increase the level of risk when you feel comfortable, and experiment with every technique you learn.

Body Awareness

Understand that it is important to eat properly and to drink fluids to hydrate your body, both before and during a ride. By properly stretching and warming up, you will reduce the risk of stressing the components of your body. All of these efforts will enhance your performance and your satisfaction with the sport.

Mechanics

Respect your equipment by maintaining it to a sound standard. Learn the basics of bicycle mechanics and carry the right tools. An improperly outfitted tool kit is worthless, when you find out too late that the wrenches you carried along don't fit the bike. Acknowledge your machine's capabilities and don't go beyond them. Riding allows you to evaluate the limits of your machine.

All of these areas are discussed in depth elswhere in this

And after...

book. They are intended to expand your understanding of respect — for yourself, your bike and the necessary techniques for safe, and enjoyable riding.

Environmental Respect

Imagine you have the newest state-of-the-art bicycle. It is every fat-tire rider's dream to have a bike like that. You started a great ride at 8:00 a.m. and traveled forty-five miles on an old logging trail. You crossed through a huge mountain meadow that was flush with color from alpine flowers. You had lunch in a cathedral of pines and watched the sunlight filter through the needles of the trees above you. You followed a long trail alongside a pristine mountain stream.

Back home, you relive the ride as you lock your bike up to the front porch. You go into the house to relax. An hour later you are awakened by sounds outside. You run out to see your bike stripped of its parts. A dark sedan with tinted windows speeds down the street. You look at your dream bike. All that's left is the frame. What a drag: your dream bike has been reduced to nothing but a dream.

Now try to imagine your bike is the environment in which you ride. Instead of mechanical components being stolen, it is the groundcover of grasses and shrubs that has been violated. The speeding dark sedan with its tinted windows is the careless mountain biker, dragging his or her rear tire down a steep alpine tundra, or plowing through an estuary or wetland. In this situation, something that was whole is now less than whole.

Recreate

We have a responsibility to respect and protect the environment in which we recreate. According to the Random House Dictionary the root of *recreation* is *recreate*, which is defined as giving new life or freshness, '...something created anew, restored, physically and mentally.'

We receive both mental and physical health through mountain bike riding. The surroundings through which we ride is equally important for your health. Plants create the oxygen we breathe. Plants clean dust from the air. We revel in the crispness of the silhouettes and shadows cast by trees through which we fly. The beauty of a distant vista charges us with vitality and joy.

The bike gives us the freedom to travel into wilderness areas. The sport is such a new phenomenon that we do not know the possible environmental impact. We must always ride in defense of the environment. There is no excuse for riding in a manner that causes damage. Without respect, every person riding today could negatively alter the trails for future riders. How fair is that? How would you feel if the trails you ride on now had been trashed fifty years ago?

Our privilege to ride on open lands can also be taken away. It is our responsibility to act in a manner that is both correct and strong. Hopefully, our world is moving towards gentler times. People are yearning for respect of self and environment, to be stewards of self and land.

As mountain bike riders, we have an acute responsibility to care for what we enjoy. We need to be aware of those actions that destroy the environment, and avoid them. We must practice conservation and improvements.

Unfortunately, as mountain bike riders, we resemble those

Respect the earth: ride with consideration for plants, animals and soil.

who ride motorized all-terrain vehicles. People who ride RV's are not vandals, but the machines they ride have more potential for destruction of sensitive trails and landscapes. Our bikes have less potential, yet many people feel our machines are no different than motorized ATV's. The majority of the people who hold this view are hikers or horseback riders who use the same trails as we do.

These people have strong organizations with the ability to have trails or lands closed to our use. Perhaps they had an encounter with a mountain biker who simply rode too fast and too close to them. We need to prove to these people, by our actions of respect and stewardship, that we are responsible enough to keep the right to the trails.

The first step is to treat the hikers and equestrians with respect. They have the right to recreate in peace, not to have someone travel past them too fast, or in a manner that appears out of control. When approaching other trail users who may not realize that you are coming upon them, let them know you are there by speaking to them, not shouting. This is especially important when coming upon a horse and rider.

With horse and rider encounters, slow the bike down and get off a reasonable distance away. Let them know that

Plants create the oxygen we breathe. They protect the soil from erosion by absorbing the impact of rain drops. The roots hold the soil together when water rushes over.

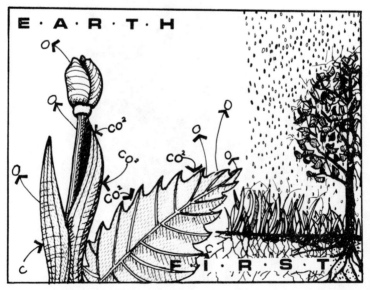

you are approaching. If the horse is not aware of your presence, speak in a soothing voice to reassure it. Allow the rider to decide if he or she needs to dismount or just direct the horse past you. A frightened horse running down a trail can be deadly to all involved. Show care.

Dogs

If you ride with a dog running alongside you, always make sure that you have full control of your pet. A dog that chases deer or tangles with mountain bikers or other wildlife is a misguided nuisance.

Respect your pet's need for shade, shelter, water and food. A dog that dehydrates on a hot summer day could be more than just a drag. Know where to get water or be sure that you or your dog carries plenty into the field.

Paying Dues

Many of the non-riding public considers mountain bikers individualists or just plain outsiders. To gain access to trails and to create our own, we must work together where and when we can.

There are many ways to pay your dues. You can join groups, clubs and organizations that are into trail improvement or construction. By banding together, you can have a voice. You can also show that mountain bikers have the ability to give. By working towards conservation of the environment, respect for fellow trail users, and self respect, you will not have to worry about having more trails closed. Some may even be re-opened.

Opportunities on Public Lands

There are many public lands still available to bike riders. The custodians of the majority of our nation's public lands are the Bureau of Land Management (BLM) in the west, and the U.S. Department of Agriculture (USDA). Maps of properties under their jurisdiction are available for a nominal fee from their local and regional offices. If they are unable to supply maps, United States Geological Survey maps are available for the entire United States.

The BLM generally is not overly restrictive At this writing, we have the right to access BLM properties where we choose. The BLM will note if mountain bikers cause damage. At some time they may become more restrictive with the use of their land.

We may not cycle on trails or lands on Indian reservations, national parks, or military bases. Individual managers of national parks do have the authority to designate trails open for mountain bike riding.

Any other public land will generally have its own regulations posted at the trail head. Even if not posted as restricted, do not assume they are open. Always check with the local parks and recreation department or the manager of the land.

Respect of Communication

All too often someone will remove a restrictive sign and claim ignorance if caught upon a closed trail. This irresponsible act further brands all of mountain bikers as outlaws. Sometimes, it is dangerous: you may face bodily harm by riding where you shouldn't. Two personal incidents come to my mind.

On one occasion, some friends and I were riding on land that was posted where the sign was gone. We came in on the backside of a stone quarry that (unknown to us) was prepared for blasting. As we were coasting downhill, enjoying the sun, the hillside beside us suddenly erupted. The explosion showered us with dust and debris. Fortunately, my friend's helmet protected him from the six-inch rock

Besides endangering yourself by riding where it is not allowed, removing a sign does not allow others a fair warning.

that glanced off his head and knocked him down.

The second incident was when a friend and I were on land next to posted property. The owner of the posted land saw us and thought we might ride onto his property. He stopped us with a shotgun to ask, "What are you doing up here?" followed by, "You had better leave or you might get hurt."

I am not saying these are typical incidents you will encounter while riding your bike. There are many other things which could cause you harm: a washed-out bridge at the bottom of a steep hill behind a blind curve; an eighth-inch cable strung across the road at neck height; a rancher pushing up a single track road with a load of hay at fifty miles an hour to reach his cattle before nightfall. All are potential pitfalls to your existence. Don't ride where you shouldn't. You might 'get hurt.' Where land is private, always ask permission to ride it. If you don't know if the

land you want to ride is private, find out.

Finding a Land Owner

You can find the land owner of property you want to ride on by checking with the county tax assessor's office. The assessor's office holds the names of all land owners in a county or parish. You will need to know the location of the property by an address, or by distances from intersections of roads or obvious topographic landmarks.

When you find out who the land owner is, arrange to meet that person. If you are unable to make personal contact, write him or her a short note listing the qualifications that should qualify you to ride there. Ask for a reply with the stamped envelope you enclosed. You will be amazed how often you will gain recreational access, if you handle these situations with tact and politeness. If there is no response, you've lost some time and a stamp. Private property is private and 'fair's fair.'

Environmental Defense

Whether riding on public or private land, always ride in defense of the environment. Please ride with the following ideas and concepts in mind. If you use them, it will show that you care for the environment.

Some areas that would not seem sensitive to unrestricted use, like swamps, bogs and deserts, really are. Wetlands and estuaries support thousands of species that are all important for our world's ecology. In arid areas, a rutted path over crusted soil can divert needed water from plants downhill and cause erosion.

Generally, the areas most sensitive to our recreation are those that are arid or swampy, or have soft organic soil. Locations with succulent plants separated by a few inches of soil between them are also highly sensitive. Don't ride across sensitive environmental areas such as wetland, tundra or saltwater estuaries. Don't take chances with environmental damage in these areas; they are too fragile. Tire ruts can cause damage to drainage as well as to the plants over which you ride. Damage to the tundra or desert can take decades to repair. It would be prudent to avoid any area that could be the habitat of rare plants or animals.

If there is an established and maintained non-posted trail, the area is probably not known to be fragile. A maintained area will have signs that warn visitors of sensitive areas. Read and heed the rules. If you are unsure whether an area could support mountain biking, find out. Call the city, county, state or federal authority and ask whether it is safe for the environment. Exercise caution where caution is due. If you stay on a trail, there shouldn't be any problem.

Waterbars guide rivulets of water over the hillside at appropirate places, where the water will do no harm. Riding around water bars causes erosion. Ride through their strong point or walk your bike across.

Trail Improvements

Many public lands and some private lands have improved trails. The improvements are usually designed to prevent the deterioration of the trail surface. Concentrated water is the primary cause of loss.

Water bars are built to prevent water damage to the trail. These erosion-control structures run diagonally across the trail. They divert water off the trail and down drainages in the hillside, where the concentrated runoff will not erode the soil. If not diverted, the water's digging action would soon turn the trail into a gully. When riding a trail with water bars, do not go around them. If constructed properly, you should be able to ride up them, preferably in the center, or through the apparent strong point of the structure. If the water bars appear weak, or you are not skilled enough to ride them, get off your bike and walk the trail.

If you ride around water bars, you are doing two rotten things to the trail. For one, you are creating a wider path by killing the plant material under your tires. With time, this exposes a route for erosion. Secondly, costs of upkeep for the wider trail will create further demands on maintenance budgets. Demands by hikers and maintenance departments to get the mountain bikers off the trail before it becomes unmanageable could be next.

Trail Adherence and Erosion

Stick to the trail. The first few times on a particular trail, ride it conservatively. You can calculate your speed for the

Cutting between trails causes a crisis in the environment. Where one bike travels, many follow, eventually causing a trail of bare soil.

next ride, helping you avoid running off the trail. Losing control could cause a crash as well as the destruction of the trail edge and the plants along it.

Never short-cut between the switchbacks of a trail. The trail has probably been laid into the hillside where the least erosion will occur. Short-cutting between the bends of a switchback causes erosion.

Erosion occurs when no vegetative cover protects the soil. One ride may not destroy the vegetation under the bike's wheels. But one ride is not where it ends. Other riders see the path the first rider made and follow it. Before long, the vegetation has been ridden over so many times that it is crushed beyond its ability to recover. The soil around the roots is compacted, preventing what life there is in the root from receiving any air or moisture. Soil particles become loose and erode due to damage from constant traffic. They start to move down the hill by gravity and water. All of this creates another scar in the landscape.

Downhill Without a Trail

If you must ride downhill where a trail does not exist, avoid a straight line down. Traverse the slope with a series of switch-backs to limit the length of a straight downhill

Avoid riding where there is no trail. If you must, zigzag up or down the ridge line. This minimizes erosion. Never ride straight down a valley where water will collect from the adjacent hillsides.

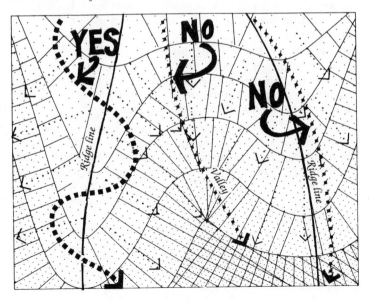

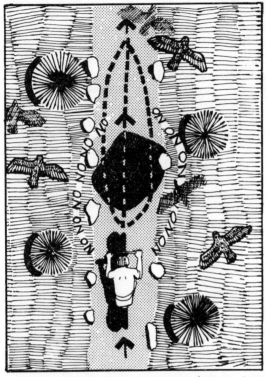

If you come upon a puddle, ride through it. Avoid going around its edge, because that would create a larger puddle and a scarred landscape.

run. This will prevent volumes of water from collecting where your tires have tracked. Zig-zag across a ridge where water will not have a tendency to collect. Riding down a valley where water naturally flows is a definite ecological mistake.

Only ride down a hill with a surface that won't be punctured or damaged by your tires. If you sink into the soil, get off the hill by walking out. Your feet may sink into the soil but the steps will not create the continuous gully that your tires would if you had ridden down.

Whether you are riding across an open hillside or down a gravel trail, always brake with rolling tires. A rolling tire is not as abrasive to the surface as one that is locked — and you will stop quicker with a slightly rolling tire than with a locked wheel.

Puddle Awareness

When you come up to a mud puddle, check it out first. Is it shallow enough to ride through? Can you place stepping stones through it? Can you go around it without damaging the plants on its sides? Try to pass without creating a wider trail.

Chapter 2
Riding Skills

Balance

Balance is an important skill. It allows you to move surely through a maze of loose rocks, or even slick ice. Balance should be practiced with every opportunity, not just on your bike. Learn while you dress in the morning. Stand on one foot and put your socks on, as well as every other piece of clothing. When you are doing the dishes stand on one foot and scrub away. Hop down the hallway or across the living room on one foot instead of walking.

Practice on your bike at stop lights, train crossings or wherever you have to stop. Use any side slope to balance while stopped. Turn your wheel so it faces uphill. With one pedal at 11 o'clock, place pressure on that pedal. The pressure on the pedal counteracts the gravity pulling the front wheel down the slope. Using only your rear brake to steady the bike while you ratchet the pedal, rocking back and forth. Keeping balance, strive to keep the wheel turned uphill so you can keep gravity on your side. To start practicing to balance, ride down the very edge of a sidewalk at the lowest speed possible. Graduate to riding the length of a 6" high curb for five feet, ten feet, and more. The slower you can ride the edge the better your balance is. You're great when you can stop on the line for ten minutes.

Riding

Riding is more than just having your legs and feet move the pedals around the crank. Pedaling can be relaxing or exhilarating. There is a scenario that allows for the leisurely cruise along a lazy river trail on a warm fall day. Or it can be a fast full-tilt downhill descent with adrenalin flowing freely in your veins. When pedaling is done correctly, there is a fluid movement of yourself and your bike, propelling you forward efficiently.

Determine the correct seat height by extending your leg in line with the seatpost with your heel on the pedal.

Take a plumb line and adjust the forward location of your seat so the line is held on your knee as shown and passes through the center of the pedal.

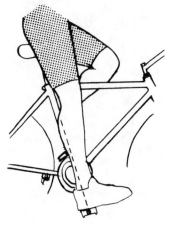

Frame Size, Seat Height and Position

Try adjusting your seat position when riding on different
trail surfaces. Evaluate the seat position by riding on a
smooth surface, either level or with rolling hills. From this
point, you can adjust your height down for trail grade or
rough conditions. Use the following advice to adjust your
seat height and position. Ride a few times with it at this
height to allow yourself to adjust to it. If the position does
not feel just right, change it.

First, you need a frame of the right size. A rule of thumb is
to have a bike with a top tube that is 2½—3 inches below
your crotch. Alternatively, you can straddle the top tube
and raise the bike until the top tube reaches your crotch.
Now the front wheel should be 5—6 inches off the ground.
However, your body's build may require a different frame
size than the one indicated. This is often the case for
people with longer than average limbs or torso relative to
their overall height. Where you can, work with a good bike
shop, one with a person who cares that you get the right
frame size. Shop at times when they are not too busy, to
get the most attention.

To adjust your seat height, it helps to have a partner
steady the bike. Sit on the bike while the other person
holds you and the bike in an upright position. Place the
heel of one foot squarely on the lower pedal and extend
your leg. The crank arm should be in line with the seat
tube. Raise the seat so that your knee is comfortably
straight but not strained. Tighten the seat binder bolt at
this height.

When the seat height is set, bring the foot to a position
that sets the crank arm horizontally forward. Move the
foot back so the ball is directly over the pedal spindle. Assume your typical riding position on the handlebars and
saddle. Have a friend take a plumb line, a string with a

To adjust the seat's
forward position, loosen
the bolt under the seat.
After locating it properly,
tighten the bolt again

weight on it, and hold the end of the string, as shown in the illustration. The string should pass the center of the pedal — if it does not, move the seat position forward or back until it does.

When the proper seat height has been set, mark its location. Use a file to lightly score a line on the seat post at the proper height. A line will allow you to return the seat to this height, quickly and easily. Do not go past the maximum height line marked by the manufacturer on the seat post. Doing so could cause an accident or damage the seat tube.

With the ball of the foot centered on the pedal, you will want to have a slight bend to the knee when the leg is fully extended when pedaling. The seat is too high if you rock from side to side when you ride. First-time riders often want to touch the ground with their feet when they start off. That's fine for the first few rides, but the position outlined above is really more efficient. You'll soon learn to dismount by sliding forward when you need to be on your feet.

Pedaling Motion

Effective pedaling should be created by a smooth, continuous flow of energy from legs to pedals. The laws of physics dictate that a smooth, continuous application of power makes the most of momentum. Changing from one speed to another takes more energy than pedaling with a constant, continuous flow of energy.

The feet should be slightly pigeon-toed on the pedals. The knees should be very close, almost touching the top tube while pedaling. This position will reduce wear on your knees. Women, because of their wider pelvic structure, need to strive for a straighter line from the hips to the feet when pedaling. The natural tendency will be for the knees to be further from the bike frame than they should be. Relieve the stress that this position will cause by drawing the knees closer to the bike.

If you are lunging on the pedals, you are constantly increasing the speed of the tire through the down stroke. Coming back up with your foot, you change the direction your foot was traveling. To change from a lunging down stroke to coming up, you slow down. This implies that lunging is not the most effective way to pedal, however fun it is. If you are interested to know the reasons why this is true, dig up a book on physics and look up *rotational motion*.

Proper pedaling uses a continuous flow of energy from your legs to rotate the pedals around the center of the crank. The spin is fluid and smooth. Keep in mind the circle of the crank as you pedal. Try to match it with the pressure you apply to the pedals. Toeclips can help by allowing you to pull up on the pedal as well as pushing forward when you are rounding the top of the stroke. The toeclips also allow you to use a different set of muscles on the upstroke than those used on the down stroke. The down-side of pulling up is that you do not have gravity helping, as you do on the down stroke. Pulling up seems to take more energy than the effort's worth. Concentrate on pushing at the top of the stroke and pulling at the bottom of it. Toeclips, however, are not necessary for a smooth spin.

The standard position for pedaling has the heel slightly higher than the pedal, as the foot rotates around the crank. This allows for a more direct application of force to the pedal. It also reduces the amount of flex to the arch of the foot when you're pushing down. If you maintain this position on long rides, you will find fatigue a companion. Using the same muscle groups in your legs over and over will stress these muscles. On long rides you will want to rotate your foot so that at times it is parallel to the ground to relieve fatigue. At other times it may be more comfortable to have the foot at various angles towards the ground. By changing the angle of the feet occasionally, you will be using slightly different groups of muscles, allowing the primary ones a rest.

Shoes

Shoes are a very important consideration. The best transference of energy from your muscles to the pedals is through a hard-soled shoe or boot. When pushing down on the pedals, a hard-soled shoe will transfer more energy. Wear special mountain biking shoes when not using toeclips. Their ribbed soles mesh with the ridges of the pedals, helping you pull back at the bottom of the stroke and push forward at the top. Especially on technical or long rides, soft-soled shoes should be avoided.

High-top boots protect your ankles from the crank arms and support them during pedaling. They are invaluable in saving the ankle from twisting and tearing when you unexpectedly dismount at high speed.

Gear Selection

The gear to use is the one that is comfortable to spin. The proper gear can be determined by the force exerted upon

Wear rigid-soled shoes to apply force most efficiently to the drivetrain. Your output is limited when you pedal with soft-soled shoes. The energy it takes to compress the sole between the bottom of your foot and the pedal is non-productive and could have been used in the pedal stroke instead.

the pedal. The force you use to pedal should be firm. Spinning the cranks at eighty or more revolutions per minute is a standard that many road cyclists strive for, in order to obtain a credible level of aerobic fitness and endurance. It is suitable for riding on relatively smooth surfaces, like asphalt or well-graded gravel roads, but on a difficult mountain trail, the pedaling rate will be lower. There will be plenty of times on uphill climbs where you will not be able to exceed thirty or forty rpm in the lowest gear; so when you can, spin at eighty.

If you maintain a constant spin of the crank through the course of climb without gasping for air at the end, you did one of two things. Either you rode the hill too casually, or you climbed spinning briskly without stressing your body. To build strength, pick a higher gear that will leave you panting at the top of the hill. Powering up a steep hill in a high gear prior to completing one whole season is not recommended. Strengthen your knees in your first season. As a general rule, remember that pushing high gears on steep grades breaks knees, while spinning low gears builds knees.

Only change gear while the pedals rotate. Shifting when you're not pedaling will only strain the derailleurs and test your patience.

Cross Chaining — A Real Don't

With every-day use, the derailleurs, the chain, and the teeth of the chainrings and the cogs will physically change during every ride. The chain stretches and the teeth wear. Improper gearing will greatly increase this wear and can make your bike unsafe.

Improper gear selection stretches your chain unnecessarily, and the teeth of the chainrings and the cogs wear faster. Unnecessary wear on the chain and gears can be avoided if you never 'cross chain.' This term refers to the improper location of the chain in relation to the gear clusters. The extreme example of this is when the chain is on the large (outside) chainring in front, and the large (inside) cog in the back.

Three things are happening in this situation that could affect your equipment and, consequently, you. When the chain is wrapped around the largest gear of the chainring and cog, it is stretched in length. The angle the chain follows between the two clusters of gears stretches the chain laterally. This angle causes the sides of the gears to wear. This wear on the teeth causes them to weaken. The ends of the teeth become thin and pointed. This wear on the sides of the teeth is caused by the chain's change in angle. The chain is in a straight line as it comes around the large cog in the rear. It then angles to the front chainrings, forming a straight line again to go around the chainring. The chain links also rub along the sides of the teeth as the chain angles from the cog to the chainring, weakening it.

The chain should mesh smoothly with the teeth of the chainrings and sprockets. The distance between the links of a stretched chain becomes longer than the distance between the teeth of the gears. This does not allow the chain to mesh with equal pressure on each tooth that it engages. When equal pressure is not applied to each tooth, there is a greater possibility for a slipped chain or broken tooth.

If you need to jam the trail, a stretched or worn chain can cause disaster. It may slip from the gears because of their improper mesh and the pointed teeth could allow the chain to roll off and the width of the teeth could be reduced to the point where they might break off. When you are putting all of your energy into a down-stroke and a tooth breaks or the chain slips, the likely outcome is a crash. The result could be extreme, especially if you are on narrow boulder-lined trail.

The proper relationship of the chain to the gears is the straightest line. Never select gears where the chain runs from big to big or small to small. Select the gear so that

Do not cross-chain. The two lines show improper chain locations between chainrings and cogs on the cluster.

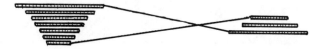

the chain forms a near-straight line between the cog and the chainring in use. If you are on the small (inside) chainring in front, use only the inside three inside cogs. If the chain is in the middle chainring in the front, use the three center cogs. If the chain is on the outside chainring, use the three outside cogs.

To test for a stretched chain, use a ruler to measure from the center of one rivet to the center of another. Twelve links should measure twelve inches (see the illustration for a definition of one full link). Replace the chain if it is stretched more than $\frac{1}{8}$ inch over twelve inches

Shifting While Riding Uphill

Shifting the gears can be a real pain if you are on an uphill climb and find yourself in a gear that is too high. Shifting down can be difficult because of the stress that is on the chain. The derailleur may not have a enough strength to change gears effectively.

Always try to downshift before the hill. Easier said than done. One technique will help in that awkward situation of making a gear change on a uphill grind. Give a concerted push with the pedals so you surge uphill for a moment. While you are in that surge mode, pedal to turn the gears, but not so much that you engage the rear wheel. The moment of relaxed tension from easing up on the freewheel will allow you to shift. On flat rides, if you ease the pressure on your pedals while shifting, you will prolong the life of your derailleurs and other components.

Riding Uphill

Riding up a steep hill challenges your prowess in the pedals as well as your ability to plan. As you approach a long hill, your throat may become parched by the time you get

Worn teeth look like shark's fins and are potentially dangerous as well. Never ride with teeth that resemble this shape.

to the top. If you planned ahead, you will have taken a healthy drink of water before starting the ascent. If you haven't, you may need to stop further up. On really long steep hills, you will probably need a drink at some point anyway. If you are unable to grab the water bottle and maintain your forward momentum, look for a flatter spot in the hill where you can comfortably stop.

Another option is to stop near a rock or something else projecting from the surface of the trail. Place your rear tire on the uphill side of the obstruction. This will prevent you from rolling backwards when you start again. You also have an easier push-off from this spot. To start, have your stronger leg at the top of your power stroke. Engage your rear brake until you are ready to start pedaling. Stand up on the pedal and coordinate the release of the brake with the beginning of your power stroke. The other foot should be firmly planted on the surface of the trail. This foot is pushing you and the bike forward as you take the first downstroke on the pedal with the other foot.

Lower and center your body over the frame as you apply firm, smooth force on the first pedal stroke. This will keep the rear tire from spinning and the front tire on the ground. If your weight is placed properly, the front tire will graze the surface of the trail, enough to allow you to steer. This will also present less resistance to your start.

The second stroke down is just as important, and slightly more difficult. It is a matter of placing your foot squarely upon the pedal while continuing the smooth application of power. If you ride with toeclips, don't worry about putting the foot in the clip immediately. In time, you will develop the ability to tap on the second pedal to turn it the right way round and enter the foot under the clip with ease after you have started uphill.

When you start uphill, your body should be in a position that could be described as 'squat-standing.' You are bent forward at the waist, your rear is near the front of the seat, your knees are more than slightly bent. Once you have started, you will want to maintain this squat-stand-ing position as long as necessary to gain momentum. When you can, sit back on the saddle, keeping your weight centered over the bike. Sitting on the seat and pedaling takes less effort than standing on the pedals.

In the following paragraphs, I have summarized some more tips that will help you climb those major thigh-bust-ing hills.

☐ When the traction is sure, ride with your weight equally upon both tires. When you come upon an obstacle, shift your weight back as the front tire meets it. Once the front tire is over the obstacle, pedal the rear tire up and over. Sometimes it is helpful to hop the rear wheel up and over.

☐ Keep a loose grip on the handlebars. Don't waste energy by clamping down when it is not necessary. Save that energy for pedaling. Relax every part of your body that isn't needed to get up the hill.

☐ Raise or lower your seat to a comfortable height. Your weight will then be in a more useful position to gain traction. Do not lunge from side to side as you go up, as the lateral motion may cause you to lose traction, as well as sapping energy needed for the next hill.

☐ Use visualization. See yourself making it to the top of the hill with the power and strength required. If the hill is extremely long and steep, don't look up. Focus on the trail in front of you; this will make it easier to plan your 'line of attack' around obstacles. Develop a smooth rhythm, balancing your power output to your breathing.

Carrying the Bike

Sometimes, you'll just have to carry the bike uphill. You can't avoid it, especially if you are into adventure and exploration. It's a good technique to use when the hill is too steep to ride. Besides getting where you want to go, you can enjoy the scenery as you trek up.

To lift your bike without strain, stand alongside it with your hand under the top tube (palm up). Find the center point of your bike and squat down and wrap your thumb and fingers around the top of the tube. Your elbow will be within the triangle of the top tube, seat tube and down tube.

Steady the handlebars with your other hand to prevent them from turning back and bruising the hand that is supporting the bike (on the top tube). From this position, as you lift with your legs, your back is doing very little work. Allow the bike to slide forward so that your shoulder is in the bike sling (if you have one) or with the top tube resting lightly on, or near your shoulder. Up the hill you go. If you are in a hurry, hold onto the handlebars with one hand, the other hand gripping the rear of the seat. Then, run with the bicycle rolling alongside you.

Riding Downhill

Nothing else is quite as exhilarating as a quick descent.
Your knees are bent, absorbing the vibration from the surface under the tires. The lowered seat allows you to lower
your center of gravity when sitting, making for a more
stable riding platform. The steeper the downgrade, the
lower the seat should be. Position your body over the rear
tire, a requirement for stability and quick stopping.

Scanning

While descending, even at the slowest speeds, you should
still be looking ahead, deciding how you are going to ride
the section of trail — just like when skiing or driving. *Scanning* is a series of quick eye movements between points
just in front of the tire and some distance ahead of it. You
should scan further down the trail as you speed up.
Peripheral vision does double duty, looking for loose rocks
or gullies that may cause a problem. You can plan a quick
hop to avoid a rock or a perpendicular gully eroded across

Place your weight behind the seat and near the rear wheel when traveling
down steep terrain, rocks or water bars. Use the front brake very lightly and
hope your hand does not have an anxiety attack.

the trail. Efficient and safe scanning of the trail is accomplished through practice.

Handlebar Vibration and Tire Pressure

On long descents over a washboard surface, the vibration caused by the trail sometimes causes an itching sensation in the surface of the arms. One way to combat this is to wear padded riding gloves. Another way is to keep a very loose grip on the handlebars. Keep the grip firm enough to maintain control, but allow the handlebars to vibrate within the circle of your grip. A third way is to let some air out of the tires. The bike's impact on the rippled surface will be greatly absorbed by the tires' lower pressure. However, never go below thirty pounds per square inch in the tires, since the tires will not respond with a healthy bite, and rims and tires will be more susceptible to damage. Riders who are heavier than average should use proportionally higher pressures than those suggested above.

On trails with rocks or other debris projecting from the surface, do not have less than thirty-five pounds of pressure. Upon impact, tire tubes can be pinched between trail debris and the rim, and this will puncture the tire. The proper pressure also prevents damage to the rim.

A safe pressure for descents depends on the terrain and your riding technique. A good starting point would be around forty to forty-five pounds of pressure in the tires.

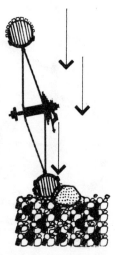

Left: Tire pressure is an important factor. Too little pressure may cause the tube to be pinched and damaged between the tire casing and the rim. Too much pressure will cause the bike to vibrate severely on bumpy trails
Right: A tire pressure that is too high may lead to instability. Trail riding with a tire pressure between 35 and 45 psi provides a happy medium under most circumstances.

At this pressure, the tire will absorb impact, it will not be so hard that the vibration causes loss of control. This pressure will also prevent a pinched tube or a dented rim.

Although more air pressure in the tire prevents a pinched tube, you do increase the risk of losing control on a bumpy trail. The harder the tire, the more it is going to bounce. The more the tire bounces, the less time the tire makes contact with the ground.

Other Tips

When riding downhill on bumpy ground, lower the seat three or four inches. Stand on the pedals with your knees flexed to absorb the bike's vibration and grip the seat between your thighs. This will allow you maximum control of the bike.

When traveling downhill on a narrow trail cut into the side of a steep hill, keep the uphill pedal up. You'll be less likely to have the pedal hit the side of the trail or catch debris.

Power Out of it

Many riders abandon their bikes too early when riding in loose gravel, snow, or a steep incline. They fear a loss of control. *Fear* is the key word here. If you stay with the

Low tire pressure increases rolling resistance because of the greater contact surface area. On the other hand, you get badly needed additional traction in sand, snow or loose trails on uphill runs. A higher pressure in the front tire minimizes rolling resistance in the front. Lower rear tire pressure maximizes traction.

bike and use power combined with body language, you can ride out of many situations. Sometimes fear will stop you where an obstacle would not.

With snow, the front tire collects snow in front and under it. This is due to a lack of traction where the tire meets the snow. The wheel slows down, snow builds up in front of the tire which then causes the front tire to slide. In gravel or sand, the tires sink or turn. When climbing an incline, debris or loose gravel may stop the bike. All these situations lead to loss of control due to diminished ability to steer a straight line and maintain balance, and loss of forward movement.

In many cases, a little torque to the pedals and body language will get you out of these situations. Get the front wheel up so it can pass over the obstacle. Apply a concentrated push on the pedals, and pull back on the handlebars with your arms. Throw your torso back and slightly down. What you are doing in essence is pulling a little *wheelie.* Once you've done this, stay on the pedals and power out. If you start to lose your balance and lean to the right, turn right so that you can use the bike's lean and steering direction to regain your balance. If you lean to the left, turn left and lean right.

You can stay with the bike when you might otherwise believe you can't. Practice in these situations is your proof that you can often finesse out. Just try it. If you dump the bike, the damage done will probably be no more than if you had quit at the beginning of the trouble.

Route Surveying

On a long cruise, conserve energy. Allow yourself to have the strength necessary to reach your destination. Plan the smallest detail of your route as you ride. Steer your bike to avoid tackling the larger obstacles in the trail. Trying to surmount all those logs and rocks can really sap your energy. Pick your path to take advantage of the firmest surface of the trail; usually, that is the higher portion of the road. Respect water bars — don't go around them

The low speed of an uphill climb requires accurate steering. Accomplish this with the proper weight on the front tire, the minimum necessary to steer the bike. This also reduces the pushing of the front tire through loose trail surfaces. Your rear tire drives through the stuff.

Braking In General

Effective braking is achieved by the brake pads gripping the rim of the wheel. If the tension on brake cables is not

enough, braking effectiveness is decreased. Test the gripping ability of the pads on the rim by riding at a moderate
speed on a concrete or asphalt surface. If the wheels skid
when you brake hard, the system is working well. Wet or
dented rims, and those that are severely out of true severely limit brake performance.

Dented rims should be repaired or replaced. Even a small
dent in the rim will cause undue stress on the brake arms
when the pads hit the dent. Weakened metal may snap,
causing a potential crash situation. Wheels out of true will
wobble, causing the brakes to alternate pressure between
left and right brake pads. This is not an efficient way to
stop a bicycle.

As a mountain bike rider, you will at times be riding in
rain, sleet, snow, and through mud puddles. To stop
quickly with slime on the wheel is almost impossible. Always squeegee your brakes when you are riding under
those conditions to remove excess moisture. That is done
by lightly applying the brakes as you travel down the trail
or road. Ride the brakes to help keep the rim free of excess
water.

When it's raining, you may have to ride the brakes con-
tinuously. Yes, that wears on the pads and it takes extra
energy to pedal your bike. Yet your need to stop far ex-
ceeds the potential cost of wearing your brakes down or
the extra effort required to reach your destination.

After riding through mud or even a puddle, check the
brakes immediately. Grit may impregnate the pads, preventing them from coming into full contact with the rim. If
they don't work, ride the brake to dry the rim; if that
doesn't work, clean the brake pads. When braking, lead
with the rear brake by applying pressure on it first. Then
bring the front brake into play.

The One-Brake Method

Imagine you are cruising down a very steep hill that is
loaded with curves. You come upon a switchback and
decide to slow the bike down by braking before entering
the turn. You hit the rear brake and the cable snaps.
Another scenario: you are traveling down the highway
when an accident happens ahead, right in your path.
Again you hit the brakes only to find one or the other has
failed. Or perhaps you have forgotten to connect the rear
brake cable after putting the wheel back on the bike? In
any of these cases, you are not able to stop the bike by
dragging your foot, as the speed is simply too high. If you
have not practiced in a controlled way, you may apply the

front brake too severely, causing you to tumble over the handlebars.

Practice stopping your bike with one brake. The position of the body is different, depending on which brake you apply. With the rear braken, the torso position should be low down and far back, your rear end over the rear wheel, arms straight and nearly locked in a straight line. When braking with the front wheel only, hold the arms nearly locked to prevent the front wheel from turning and keep your rear end over the rear edge of the seat. Keep your weight low and apply the brake in a smooth and firm manner. First practice at very low speeds until you understand the dynamics of stopping with only the front brake.

Stopping with just the rear break does not require quite as much intense concentration as braking with the front only. In either case, though, start practicing by braking from slow speeds and increase the speed as your ability increases. Practicing this skill should be safe and comfortable. It is important to understand how fast you can stop with only one brake.

Downhill Braking

Accomplish braking on a downhill run by working both the front and rear brake. Never lock the brakes. A locked brake will pile loose trail material up and under the tire. A slowed but still rolling tire will stop you quicker than a locked brake. It allows the tire to roll over the debris that would build under a locked tire. While you slow or stop your bike, avoid going over the handlebars by keeping your weight back. Gravity becomes your tool.

Before starting a long downhill run, lower the height of your seat. This allows you to move easily behind the seat, with your rear only inches above the rear tire. The lower center of gravity allows for stability while maneuvering. Moving your mass towards the rear of the bike provides a better weight distribution when braking.

If your weight is forward, your mass is transferred to the front by your forward momentum. With your weight upon the front wheel, your braking potential is reduced. Of the two wheels, the front one is the least stable. It can turn left or right while braking, causing you to lose control.

Stopping Really Fast

The fastest way to brake is described as power braking. Imagine you are cruising down a mountain trail and a deer suddenly appears in front of you. You're not scared you'll hit her because she may simply leap out of your way. If she doesn't, you can always power-brake to a complete stop in a matter of a few feet.

This technique should be used rarely, as it has the potential to be destructive to the environment. It really digs the tires into the ground. Use it only when your safety is threatened, when your life or limbs depend on your ability to stop. The best place to practice this technique is on maintained gravel roads. You will not damage those roads when learning this important skill.

Power braking is a dramatic leap (with your feet remaining aggressively on the pedals) backwards and down. You firmly and assertively apply both brakes in a smooth and solid motion. Slightly more pressure is applied to the rear brake. Keep your weight centered behind the seat. Stop with your arms straight out, legs flexed and your rear just inches above the rear wheel.

Whether you fishtail or not will depend on the surface on which you are braking. The rear wheel should not come forward, along your side, causing a lateral slide on paved surfaces. This is the most stable way to stop fast on any surface except ice.

Braking on Ice

On ice, ride slowly and conservatively. It is very unpredictable. Keep your seat low: this will allow you to drop both feet easily to the ground to avoid a spill. Practice braking in any area where there is not much to crash into. Wear a lot of padding, in the form of several layers of clothing, to help absorb the impact in a fall. Always wear a helmet.

First try braking from low speeds. Apply more force to the rear brake than to the front. Again, the front wheel is the least stable of the two. The rear wheel essentially acts as a rudder that will help you stop in a relatively straight line.

One trick that is fun to practice is pedaling at a very slow speed and then slowly applying the front brake. The front wheel is barely turning or has completely stopped. Keep pedaling and try to keep moving forward.

These are two things you can practice when you want to mess around, so you'll understand braking on ice better. That may be to your advantage during winter riding. Think about the old Boy Scout motto, 'be prepared!'

Hopping the Bike

Imagine you are riding down a steep hill. The trail surface is packed gravel. You are traveling at a speed that allows you to control the bike, yet fast enough to feel the adrenalin flush in your veins. Around a corner you go and directly in the middle of the trail is a jeep. On either side of that jeep are two rocks, one is about twelve inches high the other two or three feet. If you were to hit the brakes you would surely lose control. What do you do? You hop the twelve inches! How do you do that? Practice.

When tackling anything that takes concentration and practice, start small. Take that twelve inch mountain and turn it into an ant hill. Bounce over the ant hill and move to something taller. You need to feel totally comfortable on your bike. If you are not, don't try hopping until you are. Comfort means you know how to fall in a manner that preserves your life and limbs. Balance is a way of life.

With your comfort level high, start bouncing the front tire on smooth asphalt. Stand on the pedals with about a third of your weight on the handlebars. The way to start is by pushing down with your weight on the handlebars in a very quick motion. Simultaneously push down on the for-

In case of unexpected events, an immediate stop from any speed can save lives.

ward pedal and then lift your weight up by raising your torso quickly at the waist and pushing away from the pedals with your feet without leaving the pedals. You are releasing your weight off the bike. This allows the tires' compression to spring the weight of the bike itself back up.

Think of this as springing off from a diving board with the compressed tires as the board. Practice hopping until you can raise the tire four or five inches above the pavement. When you have mastered this, you are ready to do it with both wheels.

Tire pressure is critical for hopping. With too little pressure, you will not get enough lift. With too much pressure, you will not be able to compress the tire adequately for it to spring the bike up. The required pressure varies, depending on your weight and the force you apply down. A person weighing 170 pounds might start with about forty pounds of pressure in the tires.

To stop almost instantaneously, aggressively leap behind your seat and hit the brakes. The squeeze is firm, quick and aggressive.

To jump the bike, put your weight on the pedals and stand up. Force your weight back down on the pedals. The front pedal should be slightly higher than the rear pedal. The tires are compressed like a spring by this action.

You need to experiment with the pressure to see what yields the best result for you. Try hopping with different pressures until you find the one that works for you. On the trail, your tire pressure may differ from the pressure you used to practice. The trail surface may be softer than the surface you learn upon, and a soft surface absorbs the

This is how your weight should be distributed on the down stroke: 30% on the forward pedal and 40% on the rear peadal, the rest on the handlebars.

Raise your weight off the pedals and handlebars by springing up off them. The tire decompression will cause the bike to follow you up.

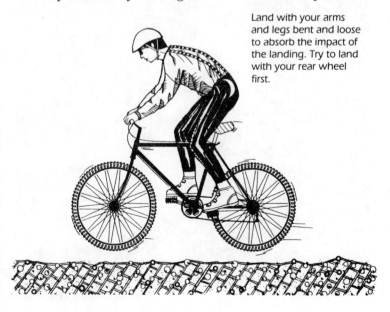

compression of the tires, thus not allowing you to spring up. Keep these two variables in mind and adjust your expectations accordingly.

To hop the whole bike, you must stand on the pedals. With the rear pedal slightly lower than the front pedal, raise up a bit with your weight. Then force down upon the

Land with your arms and legs bent and loose to absorb the impact of the landing. Try to land with your rear wheel first.

pedals and handlebars. About ⅓ of the downward force
should be on the handlebars., the rest upon the pedals,
with slightly more towards the rear pedal. Bend your
knees and stay that way.

After compressing the tires, immediately raise your weight
off the bike, allowing the tires' decompression to lift the
bike off the ground. Don't overdo the lifting off the pedals,
as your bike may not follow as far up as you. This would
make it more difficult to find the pedals again. Always

To ensure the most stable landing when flying over a jump, make sure to pull
the front wheel up slightly. Keep your rear towards the back of the bike, so you
land on your rear wheel first, and your arms and legs flexible.

Climbing steps in an urban situation (where allowed) is a good way to practice trail technique. A way to climb concrete steps is to come upon them at a low speed. Just as the front wheel reaches the first step, pull the front of the bike off the ground. The front wheel has to be high enough to clear the first two or three steps. As the front wheel hits the step, pedal through with your weight on the rear wheel to take you over the steps. But be careful: if your weight is too far back, you may flip your bicycle backwards. Time your pedaling so that your leg is in its power stroke position when the rear wheel hits the step. Learn this technique on one step first and then increase the number of steps you practice on.

keep your arms and legs flexible as you land to absorb the shock.

The first time you try it, the bike will not raise off the ground very far — if at all. The timing of moving your weight up, then down, then up again is difficult to master. You can do it, though. Once you can raise the bike up over the pavement you can start practicing over obstacles. Begin with small rocks or pieces of wood that will not

Many stunts and techniques can be practiced on your way to work and back home. Using the bike whenever you can also benefits the environment — including the air we breathe.

cause an accident if you hit them. Progressively jump higher obstacles until you are satisfied with your hopping ability.

Hopping Suggestions

Lower your seat to practice. This allows you to change your body position when required to maintain your balance.

Learn to hop without toeclips. You will understand the concept better with less of a chance of hurting yourself. Start hopping practice at low speeds. Obviously, the faster you are going, the farther your momentum is going to carry you. The key is to learn at low speeds and then graduate to jumps at higher speeds. Follow these suggestions to help avoid painful crashes.

Learn to jump different heights of barriers. Practice a greater height every few days. This will allow for a gradual learning curve, which is important for this technique. Thin pieces of wood stood on end are great for varying heights. They are less prone to causing accidents than rocks or bricks would be.

Balloons blown up to different diameters also provide the same safe practice. They add the excitement of a 'boom' when you don't make your goal. Practice with friends for that all important peer pressure and hazing. Use your hopping technique to leap over a pothole directly in your path as you ride next to others. This is always impressive, and it keeps your clothes free of muddy water thrown up by the wheels.

Practice hopping while standing still and you'll graduate to the ability of jumping sideways from the gutter to the top of the curb. When you practice this technique, just try to jump sideways on a flat surface while having very little forward motion. Then find a low curb to start with. To jump to the right, compress your tire and lean slightly to the right. When you spring up, the bike will follow. The angle you need is slight; you'll find it with practice.

Conclusion

All of these techniques are available for your use. You will develop other skills with time. They too will allow you to respond to all the environmental factors you will encounter on your rides.

To understand a skill, break it down in its component movements. Incrementally learn those pieces over a long period of time. Completing those phases allows you to combine them. Enjoy yourself!

Chapter 3
_____ Shaping up

Respect yourself. Whenever possible, incorporate the information contained in this and the next chapter in your daily routine. This way, you will be fit enough to appreciate and exploit the possibilities your mountain bike opens up to you.

Stretching on the days you don't ride will keep you flexible. You may also find more comfort in your body on a daily basis. It will always assist your performance in the pedals. Regular training, cross training and weight lifting will keep you at a high level of athletic ability. The variation of physical activity will keep all muscles toned. Falling, or avoiding a fall while riding, can stress muscles not typically used. With your muscles toned and stretched, you can avoid aches and pains. Joints that are flexible from stretching with strong muscles surrounding them are important. They will better absorb the natural impacts of

Cross-training: Climb, hike, swim, row, cycle on the road, run, do biathlon — have fun.

the sport. Care for yourself.

The body has the ability to adapt and increase its efficiency with training. Training increases both the quantity and
the quality of work. We ask our bodies to respond to goals
and we need to invest the attention and care in our bodies
to attain these goals. Exceptional athletes perform well
due to genetics coupled with training and personal care. If
you make demands on your body, consider what your
physical and nutritional base is: What have you been
eating and what type of exercise have you been doing recently?

A base is your starting point. It is your level of fitness
when you begin a new exercise program. It includes
strength, aerobic ability, rest and nutrition. Is your diet
nutritious? Do you work to maintain tone, flexibility, endurance? Do you get enough sleep? Do you allow yourself
enough time to rest and recover? Don't let your life become a daily routine of hard-driving workouts: you also
need a day or two of easy riding or rest.

Ask yourself this basic question: 'When riding on road or
trail, am I just riding or *training*?' Cyclists who always
have a goal down the road strive to go farther, faster.
Whether you are training or or just riding, there are some
basic principles that apply to both.

Doing well in both is the result of selecting flexible and
achievable goals. A goal allows you to go where you want.
Always accept that your goals may change over time —
sometimes even as you are striving towards one. Reality
dictates that. Realizing that, you can rearrange the goal
easily as the actual image of it becomes clear. The closer
to the goal you come, the clearer it becomes.

A goal might be described as *having to*, motivating you to
your highest achievement. Be (optimistically) realistic
about your ability to achieve it but allow for a margin of
error. It can be updated as situations change to allow for
those changes, and it should *never* take precedence over
'listening to your body.'

The Mechanics of Setting Goals

First, determine the grand design of your cycling program.
Fantasize, think big! List things that are readily achievable
and those beyond your grasp. Pick the goals that appeal to
you the most. For each goal, generate a list of ten small
steps that will lead you towards it.

Make each step small, something you know you can complete. This will generate many small successes, and these

translate into *motivation* for greater success. In moving towards the grand design, you must not short-circuit the small steps. Use them, they'll get you there.

Setting Low and High Goals

Determine the ideal program for one month, one week or one day.

The ideal desired program is your *high goal*, the one that would prove to yourself that you are stronger than you think. Now lower it to a level that assures you can't miss: that is your *low goal*. Most of the time, your performance will fall between those two standards. At either extreme, you have succeeded, which breeds success, and more motivation.

Rewards

The effectiveness of rewards has been well established by behavioral scientists. An animal (you) will perform in expectation of reward. For better performance, build a system of rewards for the behaviors that allow you to make your goals.

Rewards can be material and related to cycling. Anything can work that satisfies your need and makes you happy. Keep in mind that good cycling is its own reward. If you

Set a goal with a high and a low target. You win when you hit somewhere between them. Without a set goal, you'll wander in the 'lower hills.'

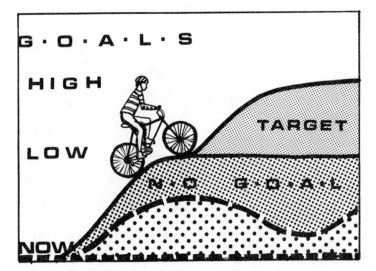

are satisfied with that statement, you already have a built-in reward system for every ride. For others, or even for the satisfied cyclist who occasionally feels old and boring, rewards can add luster to their training.

Consider the following list of rewards, or make your own: A 15-minute mental-health break. A new bicycle seat or water bottle. Frozen yogurt. Time to read your favorite cycling magazine. A visit to a travel agent to plan your mountain bike vacation. The list can become long! Decide on more rewards than you ever thought possible. Always have a way to pat yourself on the back. Beginning goal-setters should be able to generate at least 10 rewards. Aggressive amateurs should be able to come up with 25—50, while gonzo mad goal-setters can come up with 100 or more rewards.

Striking a Balance with Your Training

Anyone who mountain bikes will sooner or later run into the expression 'listen to your body.' How do you do this? It is a skill learned through trial-and-error, perfected over time. Here are some hints to help you determine whether you are overdoing it or not. Learn to distinguish normal from abnormal exercise response. Normal responses may include sore muscles, some extra fatigue (especially when beginning or when increasing mileage), some change in ap-

Abnormal training does not allow for any coasting. It is always an uphill climb. Normal training mixes rest (coasting) with hard work.

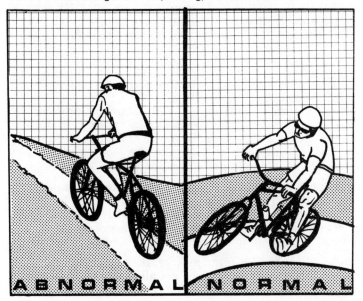

petite (be it increase or decrease), moderate muscle stiff-
ness, and associated minor aches and pains. All of the
above should be resolved the day after exercise.

Abnormal responses result from overtraining. They include the following: extreme fatigue (especially if it lingers
for several days), more frequent illnesses, pain in a muscle
or joint that begins and persists during the ride, and especially pain that lingers after a ride. Some red flags for over
training include legs that feel heavy (this is a universal in-
dicator), inability to sleep, and an insatiable appetite. It
culminates in an inability to accomplish anything except
your riding schedule. Avoid overtraining because it is deadly.

Flexibility Through Stretching

Fitness can mean many things to many people. Most ex-
perts agree that a fit cyclist must at least have adequate
flexibility, strength, and aerobic endurance to cycle at
his/her chosen level. The 'get down' mountain biker is
lean, doesn't carry extra baggage down the road, and is
flexible. However, recreational riders do not concern themselves as much with this.

Flexibility is the property that allows you to move with
ease. It allows the muscles to work without undue strain.
A flexible muscle can meet the demands of a long ride. The
potential for it being pulled in the event of a sudden, unexpected move is less. Muscles stressed by riding can short-
en over time. Lengthening the muscles with regular
stretching will allow you to maintain or improve your current flexibility. The lesson is: learn to love stretching!

How to Love Stretching.

It doesn't take long. Realize the parallel between a well-
tuned mountain bike and a fit and flexible body. Less injuries and aches and pains can be guaranteed for those
who stretch and maintain flexibility. Incorporate stretching into everyday activities. Be aware of the opportunities
you have to stretch throughout the day. Don't just reach
for an object, *stretch* for it!

Every now and then, do a long session (fifteen minutes or
more). Here is how to go about it:
You can either warm-up/cool-down with an aerobics class
or get out an exercise mat, put on the music you enjoy,
have some stretching diagrams with you, and follow them.

Stretch during a ride. For instance, during a long riding
stint, when your position does not allow you to relax, get
off the bike and do two or three stretches. It is great to

break for a stretch after you have warmed up for a while on the bike.

Here is an easy stretch to do while riding: Reach one arm back until you feel a stretch between your shoulder blades. Do this on both sides, then shake out your wrists. Stretch from the waist up and then extend a leg off the pedal. Stretching while riding will often take the numbness out of the muscles and nerves. The added benefit of a good tingle can help rejuvenate one's spirit when the ride seems long.

The Mechanics of a Good Stretch

Concentrate on the muscle being stretched in proper form. You should feel a tension in that muscle that relaxes as you hold the stretch. Assume the stretching position for 15—45 seconds, then relax. Repeat. The second time you can stretch a little farther. Sensors in the muscle that protect them from overstretching have relaxed. It is helpful to warm up the muscles before stretching by riding lightly for a while; then stop and do your 'pre-ride' stretches. This will help your immediate ride be more enjoyable.

When stretching, keep the following remarks in mind: Bouncing will stress the muscles that you are trying to stretch. Never overstretch, especially an injured muscle. Avoid all stretches that are painful. Stretching competitive-

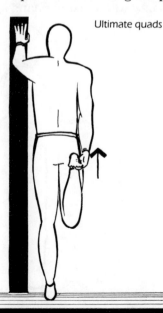

Ultimate quads

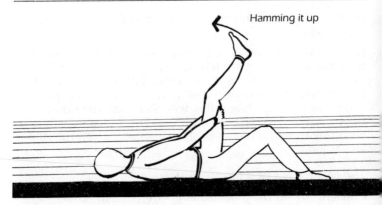

Hamming it up

ly against another person to see who can look like Gumby is a 'don't.'

The idea of stretching is to increase your range-of-motion for your riding program. Any discomfort should put up a red flag that warns you to ease or modify the stretch. Be willing to experiment with the variations until you find the stretching routine that works for you.

1. Ultimate Quads
Stand tall. Lift one foot behind you and grasp foot/ankle with hand on same side. Stretch quads gently. Do not bend forward while doing this stretch. Stand Tall! If necessary, balance with the other hand against wall or railing. If

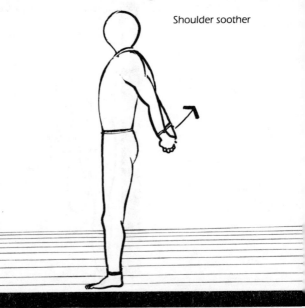

Shoulder soother

Back unkinker

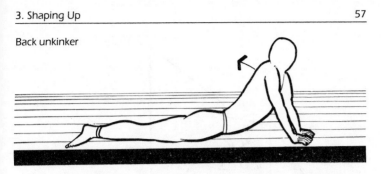

balance is good, reach straight up with other hand to stretch abdominal muscles at the same time. If flexibility is poor, loop a towel over foot to allow extra length to perform the stretch. Repeat with the other leg.

2. Hamming It Up
Lie on your back, with the small of your back against the floor, your knees bent. Raise one leg perpendicular to the floor. Maintain your upper leg position and straighten the lower leg towards the ceiling. Do not pull on your leg to achieve this position. The ultimate goal is to straighten your leg with the heel towards the ceiling. Repeat with the other leg.

3. Shoulder Soother
Stand tall. Clasp your hands behind your back. Straighten out your arms with the hands remaining clasped. Use your arm muscles to raise the hands as high as possible behind you. Do not lean forward to get your arms higher. Variation: have a partner do the work of raising your arms until you tell him or her to stop.

4. Back Unkinker
Lie on your stomach. Place the palms of your hands just in front of the shoulders (as if preparing for a push-up). Press up slowly, keeping your hips and stomach on the ground, so the back arches as the arms straighten. Be careful: this can help a normal back but may irritate a lower back injury.

Back protector (variation 1)

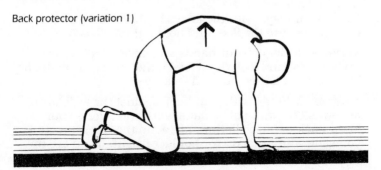

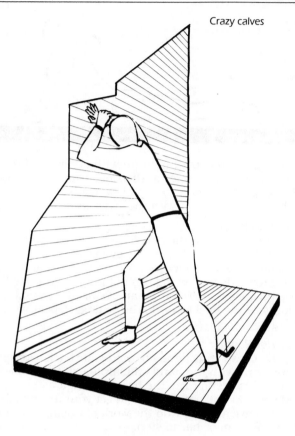

Crazy calves

Variation 1: If the former is too difficult to perform, just prop yourself on your elbows, rather than straighten out the arms.

Variation 2: This can be done throughout the day for repeated, 'mini-relief' sessions for the back. Stand, place hands on hips and lean back slightly. Sigh with relief.

5. Back Protector
Lie on your back, with the knees bent. Press your lower back down onto the floor and hold it there. Relax.

Variation 1: Get on your hands and knees. Arch your back up like a cat and look down. Hold, then relax the arch and let your back flatten out and look up.

Variation 2: Stand with your back against the wall, arms at your sides, with palms flat against wall. Press your lower back to the wall. Now, maintain that pressure as you slide your arms up to shoulder height. If you are unable to do this, it is time to work on your posture.

6. Crazy Calves
Stand, facing wall, about arm's length away. Put one foot forward with knee bent, and keep back leg straight. Hold. Then bend back knee. Repeat with other leg.

At the End of the Ride

Your muscles will be most pliable after a ride, so the best stretching can be done then. This is the time to work on your overall long term flexibility.

1. Ankle Gyrations
Sit and hold one leg up in front of you. Work the ankle in clockwise and counterclockwise rotations. Also move it up and down.

2. Foot Massage
Work all areas under and around the foot, including individual toes. Make a fist and work the bottom of the foot in a stroking motion with your knuckles. Variation: have a partner do your foot massage.

3. Wrist Gyrations
Same as ankle rotation sequence, but with the wrists. This is also a great exercise to relieve stress in the wrists while riding.

4. Hand Massage
Work your hands and the individual fingers. This is especially important if you have spent hours gripping the handlebars.

5. Finally: Polar Stretch
When you have finished stretching, lie on your back. Extend the arms flat on floor above you and reach for the North Pole. At the same time, your feet reach for the South Pole.

Balanced Strength

A well-toned, muscular body not only looks good, but helps improve riding. For instance, when your group suddenly comes to a killer climb, only the strong will survive! Balanced strength is especially important. If your strength is not balanced, one group of muscles may have developed more than its opposing group. Some benefits of balanced strength are power and protection from injury. Power is the ability to generate a high work output over a period of time. This allows you to go farther faster. Enhanced protection from injury by a strong musculature surrounding all joints is also a bonus. This helps protect the body from incurring injuries during a fall.

Added strength can be of great benefit for all mountain

bikers. The benefits of strength apply to men and women alike. Women can build strength without the bulk found in male athletes. They lack the quantity of testosterone responsible for this response. Both male and female cyclists can determine the amount of bulk they receive from strength-training. Strength-training may cause the specific muscles worked to become somewhat larger. But you don't have to be concerned about looking like a big-time wrestler.

Physiology of Strength

Applying an amount of stress that is greater than normal creates an overload, resulting in adaptation for elevated strength. Specific exercises stress particular muscles or (more often) groups of muscles that work together to produce movement. Follow strength training by an adequate period of rest for the muscle fibers to adapt and increase their contractile ability. Listen to your body. If you are sore from some hyper-activity, limit your training. Take shorter, less-stressful rides until your body says to go for it again.

Principles of Strength Training

In strength-work for the upper body, as in stretching, correct form is essential. Use a mirror and/or work with an experienced friend or trainer when starting. Learn to lift the weights with that essential form. Consider resistance and repetitions for achieving desired strength. *Resistance* is the of force applied to the muscles. In lifting, this refers to the weight lifted. *Repetitions* equal the number of exercises performed. A *training program* defines the group of exercises to be performed at a session. Maximum strength is the result of low repetitions and high resistance. This is the most stressful approach, most likely to contribute to high blood pressure responses during a workout. It is

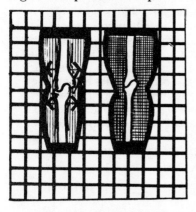

Weak muscles surrounding bones allow for movement of the bones. A strong musculature around the bones reduces the movement of bones over cartilage, preventing potential injuries.

mostly used by Arnold Schwarzenegger and his friends.

It is important to *exhale* during the resistance phase of strength exercises. Although breathing seems intuitively obvious, many beginners forget this completely. Breathe!

Moderate strength is recommended for cyclists. This is the result of moderate repetitions of higher weight (i.e. 8—12 reps), and is effective for building strength. Endurance strength is also popular with cyclists because it both adds to strength and has cardiovascular benefits. This involves moderate-to-light stress, with high repetitions (12—20). The frequency of strength exercises and stretching for the whole body should be 2—3 times per week, or every other day. Four or six times per week (i.e. almost daily) can be a program for alternating upper- and lower-body strength exercises.

Here are a few of the many ways to apply resistance for strength-training:

☐ Use your own body weight to create resistance. One advantage to this method: it is *free*.

☐ Flexible resistances, such as stretch bands.

☐ Portable equipment, such as wrist or ankle weights.

☐ Weight-training machines, such as Universal, Nautilus, or any one of the isokinetic machines, which constantly adjust to provide tension equal to that exerted by the muscle throughout its range of motion. The advantage of the machines is that their use is easy to learn and lessen the chance for injury relative to that associated with the use of free weights. Still, proper form is necessary.

☐ Free weights (barbells or dumbbells). If you do, make sure you get adequate instructions in the proper handling technique. Proponents of the free weight method

Free weights, stretch bands and dumbbells are good pieces of equipment for the home gym. Health clubs offer everything you need — and more.

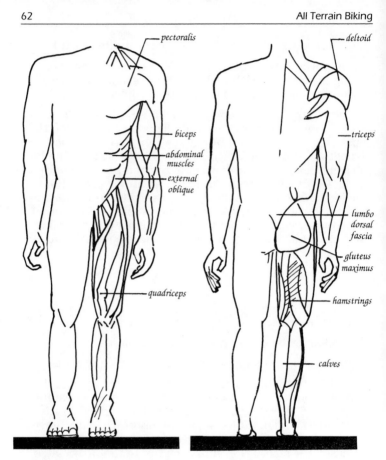

Left: The muscles and their locations as seen from the front....
Right: ... and from the back

stress that, in addition to building up strength, it improves balance and coordination.

☐ Cross-training exercises. This may not isolate the muscle groups quite as specifically, but certain sports are excellent for building strength in a particular muscle group. Occasional cross-training makes your strength workout seem more like play!

Special Strength Concerns of Cyclists

Arms and shoulders must be strong to withstand the rigors of climbing steep trails and hanging on. Many cyclists are surprised to find that it is the arms and hands, not the legs, which are sore after their first ride! Quadriceps may become much stronger than hamstring muscles. Specific hamstring exercises are necessary to balance strength and reduce chances of injury. The back quite often becomes tired and sore with cycling. Strong abdominal muscles and upper back muscles, along with a flexible lower back, will help ease this condition. The lateral muscle of the quadriceps (*vastus lateralis*) may become stronger than the medial muscle (*vastus medialis*). Therefore, it becomes necessary to work the medial, the inside muscle of this group.

The following is a suggested list of exercises you can perform to produce well-rounded strength for your cycling. It has been put into a format so that you can mix-and-match between resistance methods, as long as you choose an exercise for each of the body segments listed. The resistance methods chosen for this program include floor exercises, resistance bands, portable weights, dumbbells, and/or cross-training. No examples have been given for weight machines; simply use it for the muscle group you desire to strengthen. The instructions are on the machine. Do exercises from groups 1 through 3 during the cycling season. Add four and five during the off-season.

The primary body areas to be worked are:

☐ Arms

☐ Upper torso

☐ Hamstrings

☐ Abdominal muscles

☐ Quadriceps

☐ Calves

Muscle Group 1 — Arms and Upper Torso

Floor Exercises

1. Push-ups.

2. Push-ups against a wall. Do them standing, leaning into and pushing away from it.

3. Pull-ups.

4. Negative pull-ups. Step on a bench to clear a chinning bar, then lower your weight down. Repeat.

Stretch Band

☐ With both arms down and to one side, hold the band in each hand. Keep arms straight. Pull straight back with one arm and slowly return. Switch.

Portable Weights

☐ Use hand or wrist weights. Do the movement of 'running arms' while walking or standing in place.

Cross-training

1. Swimming.

2. Rowing or use of rowing machine.

3. Cross-country skiing or use of skiing machine.

Muscle Group 2 — Hamstrings

Floor Exercise

1. Stand tall, face the bar (or counter top). Extend one leg straight back and return. Repeat. At the end of the set, switch legs.

2. Lie on your stomach, with your hands behind your back. Keep your chest and stomach on the floor. Raise and lower your legs. Repeat.

Stretch Band

☐ Stand tall. Hook the stretch band under a sturdy table leg and around your ankle. Extend your leg straight back and slowly return. Repeat. Switch legs at the end of the set.

Portable Weights

☐ Lie on your stomach on a training bench. Attach ankle weights or hook heavyhands over your feet. Slowly raise and lower your legs (do not fully extend the legs). Repeat.

Dumbbells

1. Lie on your stomach on training bench. Place dumbbell between feet. Slowly raise and lower your legs (do not let the legs fully extend).

Cross-training

1. Pool exercises.

2. Hiking up and down hills.

3. Cross-country skiing or machine.

4. Stair climbing or stair machine.

Muscle Group 3 — Abdominal

Floor Exercise

☐ Abdominal curls: Lie on your back and bend your

knees. Cross your arms over your chest. Raise up until the shoulder blades are off the floor. Lie back down.

Variation 1: Twist at the torso left and then right

Variation 2: Elevate your legs and cross the ankles

Variation 3: Hang with hands and arms from a chinning bar with your legs straight. Raise and lower your legs.

Stretch Band

☐ Sit on a chair. Loop the band around the chair and across your rib cage. Lean forward. Slowly return. Repeat.

Portable Weights

☐ Hold heavyhands. Lie on your back with your feet in the air and the knees are slightly bent. Arms are straight out at each side. Reach up with one hand and across your body to (try to) touch the opposite foot (shoulder blade will leave floor). Return. Switch.

Dumbbells

☐ With a dumbbell in your right hand and your left hand on your waist, your back straight, bend right, then left. Switch hands.

Cross-training

☐ Swimming.

Muscle Group 4 — Quadriceps

Floor Exercises

1. Up-and-down jumps.

2. Side-to-side jumps over bench.

Stretch Band

☐ Leg extensions: Stand and hook the stretch band around a sturdy table leg. Extend leg forward and slowly return. Repeat. Switch legs at the end of the set.

Portable Weights

☐ Attach ankle weights and lie on your back. Cycle in the air.

Dumbbells

1. Partial squats without chair for support.

Cross-training

1. Mini-tramp.

2. Skiing or shredding (snowboarding).

3. Uphill hiking.

Muscle Group 5 — Calves

Floor Exercise

1. Standing, raise and lower on your toes. Variation: Stand on one leg while doing this.

2. Walk on your heels with your toes stretched skyward.

Stretch Band

☐ Hook a short band around your feet, holding the band with your hands. Raise and lower on one foot. Switch.

Portable Weights

☐ Same as with stretchband. Place weights on knees.

Dumbells

☐ Hold in hands, arms straight down, and raise up and down on both feet.

Cross-training

1. Jumping rope.

2. Climbing up and down stairs or hills.

Note: Both the quadriceps and the calves will keep strong through the actions of cycling. They should not require additional exercises unless you are going for it.

Benefits

You can get excited and feel good about the sport because it has a great deal to offer in the health and fitness department, Here is a list of the major benefits of cycling and aerobic exercise:

Long-Range Benefits:

☐ You live longer.

☐ Reduces the risk of cardiovascular failure.

☐ Allows you to reach your genetic potential.

☐ Improves your balance and coordination.

☐ Improves body composition *(muscle-to-fat ratio)*.

Medium-Range Benefits:

☐ Builds better heat tolerance.

☐ Increases ability to mobilize fat as a fuel during exercise.

- [ ] Increases muscle carbohydrate fuel stores *(glycogen)*.
- [ ] Increases aerobic enzymes.
- [ ] Increases cardiovascular efficiency.
- [ ] Produces higher $V_{O_2\ max}$ (explained in Chapter 4).
- [ ] Increases strength.
- [ ] Creates greater blood-fluid volume

Immediate Gratifications:

- [ ] Decreases negative stress *(distress)*.
- [ ] Increases positive stress *(eustress)*.
- [ ] Increases enjoyment of life.
- [ ] Creates pleasant effects of endorphin hormones produced during exercise.
- [ ] Increase opportunities to enjoy scenery, geology, flora, and fauna.
- [ ] Creates a mini-vacation during the day.
- [ ] Produces a chance to meet and ride with other great people.
- [ ] And, most of all, a good cycling program can make you *feel like an animal!*

Chapter 4
On the Bike Training
and Health

Aerobic versus Anaerobic Training

Aerobic training is exercise that is conducted at a rate that allows the body an adequate supply of oxygen. It is rhythmic, sustained, and uses large muscle groups (such as the arms and legs). It is efficient at conditioning the cardiovascular system and also burning fat.

Anaerobic training, in contrast, consists of short bursts of high-intensity exercise. Oxygen cannot be adequately supplied at such a high rate, so lactic acid is formed in the tissues. This allows the cyclist to ride at a high intensity — but only for a very limited period of time. High-intensity training is desirable for hill-climbing or speedwork, but it is not necessary for achieving cardiovascular fitness.

Have you ever wondered why some riders pass you when you are pushing a difficult grade and they are not even breathing hard? This may seem unfair, and tries the patience of even the most accommodating rider. The difference in this case is the other rider's greater *aerobic capacity.*

Physiologists measure a person's aerobic capacity as $\dot{V}_{O2\ max}$. This is the amount of oxygen an individual processes per minute, per unit of body weight. An increased $\dot{V}_{O2\ max}$ signifies a greater aerobic capacity. So two cyclists may be going at the same speed, but the one with a higher $\dot{V}_{O2\ max}$ is operating at a relatively lower percentage of his or her maximum output. What is an all-out effort for one may be

Your resting heart rate (RHR) indicates your relative level of fitness. In general, the lower your RHR, the better your cardio-vascular fitness

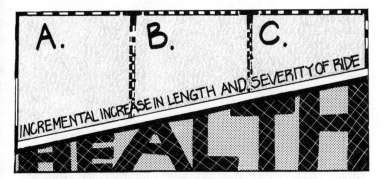

a comfortable training pace for another. On average, men have a higher $\dot{V}_{02\,max}$ than women, because women have a larger percentage of weight as fat.

$\dot{V}_{02\,max}$ may be measured directly or indirectly. The direct measurement is done by pushing a cyclist to all-out effort during an exercise stress test. This elicits maximum effort and heart rate, and is the most accurate way to gauge aerobic fitness. An indirect assessment is done by giving the cyclist a submaximal exercise stress test. Heart rate response is elicited to several workloads, and from this, the maximum level of work achievable is extrapolated. With either type of test, experienced cyclists will get better scores if the test is done utilizing cycling exercises, rather than a treadmill or other means.

According to the American College of Sports Medicine, a maximal exercise test is recommended before beginning a training program for men over 40 and women over 45. Sedentary individuals over age 30 should have a maximal stress test before starting. At any rate, you should obtain your doctor's approval before beginning any new exercise program.

It may surprise you to know that it doesn't take much exercise to achieve cardiovascular (CV) condition. The minimum recommended amount is 20 minutes, 3 times per week. A more vigorous program entails 45—60 minutes, 4—6 days per week. Above this amount, there is a point of diminishing returns for your efforts. Additional training will improve your condition up to a point. Remember to listen to your body. Ride energetically. Approach long-distance riding gently, and in a systematic fashion.

Training Intensity

The other consideration with your cycling is the *intensity* of the training. This is calibrated by taking your pulse during the ride. The recommended range for conditioning for most cyclists is 60—75% of maximum intensity. *Maximum intensity* is the heart rate when it just can't beat any faster, referred to as MHR (maximum heart rate). After becoming conditioned, the cyclist may decide to apply a higher training intensity, and train at 70-85% of MHR. It is important to budget intensity. A little bit of it goes a long way and high-intensity training may imply overtraining.

Intensity is calculated by using the *Karvonen formula.* First, find your maximum heart rate (the highest heart rate from a maximum stress test). This can also be estimated to be 220 minus your age. Calculate according to the following steps.

Karvonen Formula

1. Establish your maximum heart rate (MHR)

2. Subtract your resting heart rate (RHR), i.e. your pulse taken for one minute at rest, preferably upon waking in the morning

3. Multiply the resulting number by your selected training intensity. For instance, if you are planning to train at 60%, multiply by 0.60.

4. Add your resting heart rate (RHR)

5. The resulting number equals the heart rate you should achieve during exercise

Simplified Karvonen Formula:
THR   = RHR + TI (MHR − RHR)

where:

THR   = training, or target, heart rate

MHR   = maximum heart rate (220 − age)

TI   = training intensity

RHR   = resting heart rate

This can be expressed as follows:

THR   = RHR + TI (220 − age − RHR)

Calculating a Range MHR

As an example, we shall calculate the required MHR for the range between 60% and 75%

Lower Target:
RHR + 0.60 (MHR − RHR) =
_____ + 0.60 (_____ − _____) = _____

Upper Target:
RHR + 0.75 (MHR − RHR) =
_____ + 0.75 (_____ − _____) = _____

Let's do an example for a 30-year-old with a resting heart rate of 60.

1. Find MHR: 220 − 30 = 190

2. Subtract RHR: 190 − 60 = 130

3. Calculate Lower Target: 60 + (.60 x 130) =
    60 + 78 = 138

4. Calculate Upper Target: 60 + (.75 x 130) =
    60 + 98 = 158

Beginners and casual riders should select a training intensity range of 60—75%. The aggressive amateur can train at an intensity of 70—85%. The gonzo mad rider will probably do most of his or her training at 70—85% intensity and may at times choose to ride at 90% for short periods of speed or power work.

During exercise, there is a linear increase in heart rate in proportion to output, up to the point of maximum rate. For any given work load, it takes the heart about 3 to 5 minutes to plateau at a new rate. Therefore you should wait at least this long after you start into your ride before taking an exercise pulse. You may take either your *radial* pulse (at the wrist, just below the thumb) or the *carotid* pulse (below the jaw, on the side of the neck). Palpate pulse with the first two fingers of one hand.

The exercise heart rate should only be taken for a brief period of time. As soon as you stop to take your pulse, you begin to recover and the heart rate slows. Take a 10-second pulse, with the first beat you feel counting as 'zero.' To simplify the math, divide your training heart rates by 6 ahead of time. You will know what your 10-second pulse should be.

When riding in variable terrain, try adjusting your gearing to keep the effort of the ride fairly constant. Granted, rough terrain is often difficult to compensate for with just gear changes. Aim to keep the major part of your ride within the selected training intensity zone for your heart.

The resting heart rate (RHR) will tell you something about your level of conditioning. With training, the heart increases its stroke volume (the amount of blood pumped by the heart during each beat). A well-conditioned heart beats more slowly. Untrained individuals commonly have RHR's in the sixties or seventies, whereas a well-conditioned cyclist may have a heart rate in the fifties. Lower rates in the forties and even thirties are not unheard of.

The RHR should be taken after a period of rest, ideally in the morning when you first wake up. Over the weeks of training, it should begin to drop. You can also learn about your fitness level from your recovery heart rate. This refers to how quickly your heart rate drops (recovers) post-exercise. The fitter you are, the more quickly your heart rate will drop. Start by checking your 2-minute post-exercise heart rate to see how you are doing. One experiment to gauge the variation in aerobic fitness between you and a partner is to stop partway into the ride and both take your pulse. The person with the lowest exercise heart rate wins!

Some cyclists find that they can most accurately assess their pulse during riding with the use of heart rate monitors. Although expensive, these help you keep within your predetermined heart rate range. They have the added advantage of measuring your pulse while you ride. You don't have to concern yourself with the drop in the heart rate while taking it.

Here are two other simple put fairly reliable methods for assessing the intensity:

The Talk Test:
If you are within the aerobic range, you should be able to talk to your cycling partner during the ride.

Rate of Perceived Exertion:
If you are training at an aerobic intensity, you should be able to describe the cycling workload as 'somewhat hard' or 'hard,' not as 'very hard.'

Physiological Adaptations to Aerobic Training:

Here is a list of the effects of aerobic training:

☐ The body can consume more oxygen.

☐ Muscles have more mitochondria (the cells that burn oxygen to supply energy to the muscle).

☐ Increased $\dot{V}_{02\ max}$.

☐ Increased capillarization (the ability to transport a greater volume of blood).

☐ Higher hemoglobin value (oxygen-carrying capacity of blood). Increased aerobic enzymes (capable of doing metabolic work to sustain your exercise).

Longevity and Aerobic Exercise

Until recently, the only claim that could be made is that exercise increases the quality of life. We could not be sure about quantity. In recent years, evidence is emerging that suggests an increase in the 'quantity' of life as well: those who train aerobically and continue to do so are likely to live longer. A Harvard Alumni study (conducted over 20 years) has shown that people who exercise regularly on average lived 2 years longer than the non-exercisers.

The increase in aerobic capacity with training is greatest during the first few weeks of training, as you have farther to go. Over an extended period of training the improvement is more gradual. The bad news, however, is that aerobic capacity drops off rather quickly when you stop exercising. You can't train now to store up fitness for later! Within a period of days, the levels of aerobic enzymes drop off, and within weeks, the heart exhibits a lesser stroke volume. Several weeks of detraining will lead to significant losses in aerobic ability. But, take heart, literally. Once you have become trained, it is much easier to achieve the same a second time around. Or perhaps the training just feels less stressful.

The Big Picture

With training, you must consider the big picture. Racers train in cycles of years. With this approach, many see improvement over a period of years. Of course, there is some drop-off in aerobic capacity with age, most of it due to inactivity associated with aging, not the aging itself. Also in your favor is that competition, or just riding well, is attributable to more than just a high $\dot{V}_{02\ max}$. A cyclist with good riding technique rides more efficiently and uses less oxygen over a given distance than an inefficient rider. Other physical capabilities that one can add to riding include muscular strength, coordination, and agility.

Cognitive processes are also an important part of cycling performance. Often, experienced cyclists can ride better than others who may have higher fitness, because the experienced rider has the following features in his or her favor:

☐ Knowing how the body will respond.

☐ Knowing how to adapt to local conditions.

☐ Ability to psych out competitors (or fast partners).

☐ Correct timing of maneuvers.

☐ Interest and variety in the cycling program to keep it alive for years.

Training Specificity versus Cross Training

Training and muscular adaptations are highly specific. Consequently, to be a better rider, you must ride. To ride a mountain bike well, you must train by riding a mountain bike. An individual with good aerobic capacity can perform in a variety of aerobic sports. However, specific neuromuscular skills are different for each discipline.

Why cross-train then? The weather doesn't always permit you to cycle outdoors (mad riders, please ignore that comment). If you have limited time to ride, you may need to do other exercises to maintain an aerobic base. It will also decrease your chances of injury. Doing any one activity exclusively is more likely to result in injury. (From overuse of a particular muscle or joint, muscular imbalance, etc.) A variety in the training and exercise program helps to maintain excitement.

The most specific cross-training activities for mountain bike riders are:

☐ Riding a road bike where it is intended to be used, on a road.

☐ Practicing on an indoor bike trainer or a stationary bike.

   Use of a stair machine (legs only, or models with both leg and arm work).

☐ Use of a rowing machine (helps to build muscular endurance in the upper arms and back).

☐ Swimming (this is also good for the upper body, plus the legs can be highlighted by using a kickboard).

☐ Running and walking, especially on trails in hilly or variable terrain (this is good for quadriceps/hamstrings).

☐ Roller-skiing or on using roller blades.

☐ Aerobics for all: low-impact aerobic classes for reducing the musculoskeletal stresses associated with this form of exercise.

☐ Mixed sports: design your own biathlon, triathlon, etc., workouts, indoors or outdoors.

☐ Use your imagination: Cross-train with other sports that make sense for your biking program in terms of aerobic benefits. Important, too, are those sports that use the same muscles used in mountain biking.

At the very least, if you don't ride your mountain bike in the 'off-season,' try to do 30 minutes of cross-training, three times per week. This way, the transition to the cycling season will not be so traumatic. Plus, continue with a base program of strengthening (especially quadriceps and hamstrings), and stretching, throughout the year.

The First Ride of the Season

First things first: Is your bike tuned up? Brakes working well? Tires in good shape?

When you undertake your first ride of the season, aim to keep the pedaling resistance low. Do not include any hill work. Ride alone or with slow (not dim-witted) friends. You are likely to dehydrate more easily than when you are in top condition, so make sure you drink enough, especially those first few weeks. Your muscles are likely to become sore after your first ride. A long warm-up, and especially a long cool-down, will help to reduce muscle soreness. A good massage, preferably by someone else, but in a pinch self-administered, at the end of your ride may be in order.

The first several rides should not be very long. Instead, do several rides of 3, 4, and 5 miles. This will allow you to pinpoint your weak areas and adjust to the cycling gradually. After several rides, you can increase your distances up to rides of 10 or 20 miles. The sky is literally the limit after that.

General Principles of the Training Pattern

Always include a warm-up and cool-down period with cycling, at least 3—5 minutes each, although longer is better. It is preferable to alternate easy and hard days of training and alternate short days of riding with long days. Try to distribute the workload as evenly as possible.

An example of an eccentric contraction is letting a weight down. Another example is when your calf pushes forward at the top of the pedal stroke.

Measure your workouts in minutes rather than miles. By your efforts, you know that one mile on a trail does not equal one on the road. Increase the number of minutes gradually. Never do any significant amount of speed or power work until you have completed a number of distance rides.

Take a day off every week, or at least do something besides cycling on that day. Do the same any other time your body needs a break.

Systems Adaptations and Muscular System

You may not notice a physical problem during a ride. A pain that occurs after a ride is called *delayed muscle onset of soreness* (DOMS). This may occur later in the day or the next day. There is some speculation that the causes of DOMS may be associated with microtrauma to the muscle fibers or to the accumulation of lactic acid within the muscles. DOMS is most likely to occur when anaerobic work is done, or can be caused by exercise that involves eccentric contractions of muscles.

Eccentric contraction refers to a contraction in which the muscle lengthens rather than shortens while developing increasing tension. For example, when performing a dumbbell curl, eccentric contraction occurs in the bicep when the weight is slowly let down from a curl. An example in cycling is when you push forward at the top of a pedal stroke. Your calf is pushing with an eccentric contraction.

Some Tips for Dealing with DOMS

Well-conditioned muscles are less likely to be affected by DOMS. Stretching, strengthening, and specific training will help prepare muscles for the rigors of riding.

During a long cool-down, the body metabolizes lactic acid that has built up in the muscles, so there is less chance for this metabolite to cause soreness. Massage may help, as may engaging in a light activity the day after a heavy training session (consider swimming).

Skeletal System

Some stress on the skeletal system from riding should prove beneficial — providing you don't fall and break a bone. Although increased bone density is primarily attributable to high-impact exercise, any exercise causes muscles to pull on bone, and that stimulates increased bone mass. This is true if dietary calcium intake is adequate, which is important to all of us as we age. Since bone mass starts to decline after the age of 35, this extra banked mass will help reduce the chances of developing osteoporosis (brittle bones).

Pulmonary System

In most individuals, the pulmonary system is already very efficient. With training, there is some increase in *vital capacity*. Vital capacity is the volume of air that the lungs can forcefully expel after a full inhalation. Residual volume is the physiologic 'dead space' of air left in the lungs after a full expiration. With training, there is also a decrease in residual volume.

The combined effect of these two adaptations is that there is greater lung power after training. There are some riders who have exercise-induced asthma, and who may develop difficulty breathing after a few minutes of riding, due to bronchial constriction. A doctor should be consulted about this. The use of an inhaler before exercise and to be carried during the ride may be prescribed. Such persons should be aware that cold-weather riding may aggravate the condition and that riding in warmer/humid weather may be easier.

Endocrine System (Hormonal)

The endocrine system allows us to adapt to stress (physical or emotional) and helps the body maintain a steady state, or *homeostasis*. This system holds a certain fascination for many athletes. It may be responsible for an 'exercise high' that is both legal and natural. In fact, some claim this as a reason for developing exercise addiction (gonzo mad riders, take note).

Insulin

The output of insulin decreases during exercise. Insulin reduces blood sugar and stops the breakdown of fats, both important fuels during exercise. Some insulin is necessary, however, to allow the cells to be able to take up and use blood sugars as a fuel.

Hormones

The body produces hormones of the type and ratios that are most effective for its own needs. Hormonal regulation is quite precise and hormonal imbalances can have drastic short- and long-term effects. For this reason, the use of hormones can not be condoned as ergogenic aids (to increase performance). Don't be tricked into thinking that if some of a certain hormone is good, then more must be better. Where the endocrine system is concerned, athletes are advised not to fool with Mother Nature.

Growth Hormone

Increased exercise causes an increased production of growth hormone. This hormone aids in mobilizing fats for use as a fuel and is also important for protein synthesis. Protein synthesis builds and repairs muscle, bone, and connective tissue.

Endorphins

Endorphins are produced by training. They are the body's response to the stress of endurance training, injury, or pain. Endorphins have their action in the brain. They are structurally similar to the drug morphine, but many times more powerful. They serve to decrease pain — and they produce a feeling of euphoria.

Adrenal Hormones

Adrenal hormones help the body counteract stress (both long and short-term) and also maintain a proper fluid balance. Epinephrine (adrenalin) and norepinephrine (noradrenalin) from the adrenal medulla serve to prepare the body for action in an immediately-stressful situation also known as the 'fight or flight' response. The heart rate increases, and the response stimulates the release of fuel substrates from carbohydrate and fat stores for quick use by the muscles. Cortisol, from the adrenal cortex, helps

A potential fight-or-flight situation. Watch where you go!

the body adapt to long-term stress. It may be called upon during periods of heavy exercise. Its actions include the breakdown of fats and proteins for fuel and the maintenance of an adequate blood sugar level. Aldosterone, also from the adrenal cortex, promotes the retention of sodium, potassium and water by the kidneys; the output of this hormone increases during exercise. Long, slow, sustained exercise will stimulate fat metabolism.

Fluid Compartment Shifts

The body is mostly composed of water. The fluid within the body is contained in the blood and in other tissue. The body is able to redistribute fluids in accordance with its needs.

Blood redistribution occurs during exercise. Blood is moved from less-needed areas (such as the digestive system) to increase its supply to the exercising muscles. Also, during a hot day, blood is shunted toward the skin to aid in cooling. This cooling mechanism can require a large blood volume, and since fluid loss is greater during hot weather (perspiration), it is especially important to be well-hydrated to keep this system working.

Fluids can move into different tissues in response to changes in temperature or altitude (as well as injury). Peripheral edema causes the swollen fingers and toes that cyclists sometimes experience, but is mostly harmless. Pulmonary edema (fluid in the lungs), although rare, is a serious problem and is considered a medical emergency. You are especially at risk of developing pulmonary edema when you have rapidly ascended to altitude, engage in heavy exercise, or have spent the previous night at an elevation above 10,000 feet. This may occur during a high-altitude ride for a cyclist who is insufficiently acclimated to the altitude. Symptoms include lethargy, confusion, and painful or difficult breathing, sometimes accompanied by a crackling or gurgling sound when breathing. The treatment for this condition is immediate descent. The condition usually reverses rapidly with descent and every foot of descent counts. To avoid developing pulmonary edema, ascend slowly, rest, and start with easy riding.

Body Composition

No discussion of physiology would be complete without a reference to body composition. A rider is generally interested in knowing how much of total weight, or what percentage of the total body, is comprised of fat. This is important because stored fat is essentially inert, and therefore it does not contribute to the work of moving the muscles when cycling. These muscles must work harder to move the extra stored fat the body is carrying.

Some fat is essential for normal functions of the body. The minimum fat needed is expressed as a percentage of total body weight. This percentage is estimated to be about 3% for males and 12% for females. Some additional fat is also recommended above these essential levels. Therefore, it is recommended that a female be about 18—22% fat and a male about 11—15%. It is not unusual for an athletic female to be 16—18% fat and an athletic male, 7—11%. These lower levels are usually the result of increased aerobic training, usually coupled with strength training and a diet low in fat. These levels are desirable, as long as the athlete has good energy for riding and stays healthy.

Although excessive body fat is not good, less is not necessarily better. The cyclist should assess where the energy level feels good and at what level he or she can ride well. Too little body fat can compromise health and performance. In general, most female athletes should not fall below 15%, and males below 5%. Body fat can be assessed by skinfold calipers. This can be an excellent technique when performed by a trained and experienced tester. Underwater weighing, although not as readily available, is the gold standard for body fat testing. This method relates the amount of water displaced by the body to the weight to calculate the percentage of body fat.

Body composition does not fluctuate as rapidly as weight. Therefore, a cyclist whose body fat level is changing only has to be reassessed every 3 to 6 months or so. You can usually tell when you are ready by the way your clothes fit.

Record Keeping

Organization and stuff? Why would you want to know about that? You just want to ride? There are good reasons to be organized and keep records. Motivation, for one, making you accountable for each day. Keeping records allows you to retrace a schedule that was beneficial or, conversely, one that resulted in injury.

Keeping records helps you assess your progress towards your goal. It allows you to monitor increases in performance; you can see greater distances covered over shorter time. It can be used to impress family, friends, and prospective employers.

Tips for Keeping a Training Record

Make sure you see the record every day. Use a calendar, datebook, or printed logbook. You can also use a record of your own design. Record something each day. Make notes about days when you didn't exercise, with comments such as 'off,' 'injured,' 'resting,' etc.

Include notes about your cross-training activities. If you have a big training goal, list it on the first page of the record. Then list it every few pages to keep it in your mind until it becomes due. Then, list the small steps to take each week and meet them.

It is a good idea to take a resting heart rate at least once a week and then list it in your training record. If you track recovery heart rates, list these also.

Beginning and casual riders should list the number of minutes ridden and the highest heart rate during the ride. Aggressive amateur riders should list the number of minutes ridden and the highest heart rate during the ride, plus the route taken. Record your energy level; score it numerically and add any other pertinent comments. Gonzo mad riders should do all of the above, plus noting the estimated amount of time spent riding per week, month and year. If you want, include notes on trail difficulty or snide remarks about riding partners. Keep notes on ecology and geology. Arrange your cumulative records graphically. You can then see at a glance how you are doing. These notes will also help recount the trail when it comes time, perhaps in a year or two, to ride it again. An odometer will help you keep track of your mileage

Metabolism

Exercise is fueled by a mixture of carbohydrate and fat. The body uses fuels selectively.

☐ At the beginning of exercise, most of the energy used is supplied by muscle phosphate and carbohydrate stores (carbohydrate is stored in the muscles as glycogen).

☐ Low-level, sustained exercise mostly requires fat as a fuel.

☐ High-intensity exercise relies primarily upon carbohydrate (as muscle glycogen or blood sugar).

☐ Intermediate-level intensity requires almost equal reliance upon the two fuels.

☐ Protein makes some contribution to exercise fuel, especially in situations of extended endurance workouts (over 2 hours) or when the calorie intake is inadequate.

The body has a huge storage of potential energy in the form of fat. One pound of fat can provide 3500 calories during exercise (the number of calories necessary for running a marathon is only 2600). By contrast, the body does not have a large carbohydrate store. For one thing, each gram of carbohydrate must be stored with three grams of water. So if carbohydrate storage were very high, you would have to carry extra body fluid — excess weight.

Endurance-trained muscles utilize fat as a fuel source better than untrained muscles. Trained muscles are also able to store more glycogen (the carbohydrate fuel source) for their use during exercise. There are two things to learn from this:

1. High-intensity exercise cannot be sustained nearly as long as low-intensity exercise, both because of fuel limitations and because of lactic acid buildup.

2. To burn fat, it is not necessary to engage in high-intensity exercise.

Chapter 5
_____ Nutrition

If you are like most riders, you probably maintain your
bike to keep it in top mechanical condition. This maintenance helps to ensure that your bike can negotiate any
challenge your outing might present. The question is: have
you put as much thought into the human machine controlling that well maintained fat-tire wonder? Nutritional maintenance is at least as important as mechanical maintenance for peak enjoyment of your tour.

Balancing Your Intake

Nutritional fitness requires the daily intake of three
dietary components: calories, nutrients, and fluids. Each
is equally important; without one, the others cannot work.
Each group is individually highlighted in this text. Balance
between the three is the key. To concentrate on one area
and not the other foresake nutritional fitness.

Calories

The calorie is a unit of heat measurement. Heat is released
when energy is created by riding, running, thinking and
even sitting at work. When more work is performed, more
energy in the form of calories is used. This is a simple law
of physics; those who work or exercise hard can eat more.

Fueling the body is not just a simple matter of providing
enough calories to support the work performed. As there
are several types of gasoline, with some providing better
performance than others for your car, calorie sources also
come in several types. Knowing which calorie sources to
eat and when to eat them can greatly increase your biking
performance.

Carbohydrates

Carbohydrates are a major energy source for working
muscles. The brain and central nervous system also depend heavily on carbohydrates to maintain alertness and
coordination. In fact, carbohydrates are so important for
maintaining basic body function that protein and fat can
partially be converted into carbohydrates to maintain alertness and coordination. Because this conversion is energy
inefficient, it is recommended that athletes eat at least
half, and up to 70 % of all calories, in the form of carbohydrate, therefore insuring that carbohydrate fuel is always

available when needed.

Carbohydrates come in two basic forms: simple and complex. Simple sugar is sugar in its most absorbable form. When consumed, simple sugars almost immediately enter the bloodstream. If you have consumed a candy bar or soda on an empty stomach, you have probably experienced the resulting 'sugar buzz.'

As desirable as quick energy may seem to be, too much readily available energy at once can sabotage the body's endurance metabolism. A large dose of glucose stimulates insulin release, which in turn stimulates increased muscle glucose uptake. The result is less glucose available for use by the brain. The brain's response to this depletion is to signal glucose shortage, resulting in fatigue, dizziness, headache, and shakiness. This phenomenon is commonly known as 'bonking.' Insulin also reduces the ability to utilize fat for fuel. Therefore, simple sugar can create a double jeopardy, as it reduces the body's access to its two major fuel sources when needed most.

A better carbohydrate source is the complex type, which consist of long chains of simple glucose molecules. Their size, however, limits their speed of digestion and absorp-

Table 5-I Simple and complex carbohydrates

Simple	Complex
Sugar	Milk
Honey	Yogurt*
Syrup	Breads*
Molasses	Cereals*
Candy	Waffles/Pancakes*
Soda pop/ sweetened selzer	Beans/split peas/lentils
Fruit juice	Potatoes
Pastries	Corn
Jam/Jelly	Fruits
'ose' products (fructose,dextrose, mannose, etc.)	Rice/Bulgur/ Couscous/ Quinoa

* If sweetened, any of these products counts more as a simple than a complex carbohydrate. Beware of supposedly 'healthy' foods such as granola types of cereals, muffins and seltzer waters. Many are loaded with simple carbohydrates.

tion. Since they must remain in the small intestine while gradually being broken down into simple sugar, their energy has a time release characteristic. Carbohydrate enters the bloodstream at a slow, steady pace, which allows blood glucose to stay stable, and simultaneously prevents brain glucose deprivation. (Table 5.I provides examples of common simple and complex carbohydrates.)

Athletes may find that intensive training increases their appetite. In fact, serious athletes can often eat twice the calories of inactive people. When one starts consuming 5,000 calories per day, that's quite a bit of food. The sheer volume of a pure carbohydrate diet providing these calories (60 cups of fruit per day) is impractical for even the most cavernous appetite. In addition, carbohydrates pass rapidly through the digestive tract. This explains why a huge Chinese meal (many carbohydrates) leaves people hungry a few hours later.

Fat

An important energy source during exercise, especially during endurance activity, is fat. This fuel is calorically dense. A lot of calories can be packed into a small volume of fat. The average athlete can maintain for about two hours on his carbohydrate stores. The average body's fat stores are enough to provide between 170 and 200 hours of exercise. Since fat is so ubiquitous, it is not necessary to boost fat intake to provide aerobic fuel. Most Americans could cut their fat intake in half and would still have plenty of fat for exercise.

Regular aerobic exercise is an important strategy that encourages fat metabolism and improves endurance. The body biochemistry adapts to regular exercise by breaking down fat, making it more rapidly available as a fuel source. The net result of better fat metabolism is that muscles can utilize more fat as fuel. This spares carbohydrate for use by the brain and nervous system. Therefore, a fit biker can maintain endurance, agility, concentration, and coordination considerably longer than one who is not.

A reasonable amount of fat helps decrease the amount of food needed by increasing caloric density. Although fat is needed in one's diet, it should not represent more than 25—30% of the calories consumed. Fat digests slowly, and this will increase satiety.

Most athletes burn significantly more calories than non-athletes. This translates into more grams of fat allowed per day for an athlete than a non-athlete (40 grams is the dose recommended for the general public). The following sections provide further information for calculating your estimated caloric need, with recommended fat intake in grams. You will also learn how to evaluate foods in the grocery store for fat content.

If biking is part of your cardiovascular fitness program, choices from the unsaturated categories should be emphasized. Olive, canola, avocado, peanut, safflower, sunflower, soybean and corn oils are good sources. Limit fats from the saturated class; examples of these are meat fat, dairy fat, coconut oil, palm oil, and hydrogenated oil — it is a prudent to limit their intake.

Caloric Need

Use table 5-II below to calculate your caloric need as a function of your sex, weight, size, age and activity level.

Table 5-II Calculation of caloric need

Males			Females		
		66.5			655.1
add 6.3 x weight (lbs)	+	___	4.3 x weight	+	___
add 12.7 x height (in)	+	___	4.7 x height	+	___
deduct 6.8 x age (yr)	−	___	4.7 x age	−	___
Basal energy use*		___			___

If you are:	Multiply by:	
Sedentary	1.25	___
Training 3—4 times per week	1.5	___
Training more than 5 times/week	2.0	___

* Basal energy is defined as the body's energy turnover.

For workouts lasting longer than 1 hour, add 250 calories per half hour of exercise to your basic calorie need. For example, a 6'0" tall 180 lb 40 year old male training 3 times a week needs 2,764 calories on a normal day. On a day with a three hour ride, 3764 calories are required.

Recommended Fat Intake

The recommended fat intake can be calculated as follows:

F = ECN x 0;25 / 9 =

Where:
F   = Fat in grams

ECN   = Estimated caloric need
0.25   = Portion of caloric need taken as fat
9   = number of calories per gram of fat

For example, the same male could eat approximately 105 grams of fat per day with 25% of his calories as fat (more than twice the recommended daily dose).

3764 x .25 = 941 calories
941 / 9 = 105 grams of fat

Compare the nutrition information on all food packages. Take for example, two percent milk:

Serving size	1 cup
Calories	125
Carbohydrate1	2 grams
Protein	8 grams
Fat	5 grams

Multiply grams of fat by 9, then divide by total calories:
5 grams of fat x 9 = 45 fat calories
This is 45/125 = 0.36, or 36% of total calories.

Protein

In addition to providing material for building muscles, protein can be a significant energy source during exercise. Even with a high carbohydrate diet, most individuals deplete carbohydrate stores approximately two hours into a workout. Protein can be converted into glucose if needed, helping to maintain blood glucose and neuromuscular function. In fact, in endurance exercise, 10—15% of available fuel comes from protein. Athletes who eat a high

Table 5-III — Sources of protein

Beans, lentils, split peas	Eggs
Nonfat milk	Beef*
Nonfat yogurt	
Cottage cheese	Lamb*
Fish	2% milk*
Chicken (no skin)	Whole milk*
Turkey (no skin)	Cheese*
Venison, elk, buffalo	Duck*
Peanut Butter	Goose*
Tofu	

* Denotes foods with a high fat content

carbohydrate meal with little or no protein often find that energy levels and coordination are fine until about an hour before the next meal — that's when the 'bonk' sets in.

Make sure every meal contains a protein source! If there is a carbohydrate and protein source, you will have a steady energy level between meals. It's a good way to make sure your energy level lasts for four or more hours after a meal.

Straight Talk

If you've wondered how all of this relates to you, here is a practical guideline to ensure that your carbohydrate/fat ratio is within reason. If you remember that for every ounce unit of meat, tablespoon of fat, cup of milk, you also need to eat 3 of any of the following:

½ cup of fruit

½ cup of starch

1 slice of bread

1 glass of skim milk

For example, if you eat a typical American meal that includes a 3-ounce serving of meat, add 1 cup of rice and 1 cup of corn, plus two slices of bread, 1 cup of fruit juice, and 1 glass of skim milk. If that sounds like a lot of food, you're on the right track: Rather than eating a large piece of meat, the high carbohydrate approach would have you eat 2 ounces of meat, 1 cup of rice, a slice of bread and ½ cup of corn. Don't forget your ½ cup of strawberries, and a glass of skim milk.

Nutrients

Calories provide energy, and nutrients participate in the conversion of this energy to output. Nutrients are what

Nutrients in themselves do not give energy. They must function with foods containing calories to provide energy.

vitamins and minerals are often called. Each one has its own unique function, and when not present in sufficient amounts, that function fails. North Americans like to take nutrient supplements: 41% of us regularly take vitamin or mineral pills. It is also possible that even with this supplement, we do not meet the recommended daily allowances for all vitamins and minerals. Why is this? One suggestion is that those who rely on supplements for nutrition are lazy eaters. In other words, individuals who take supplements do not make a conscious effort to eat a variety of foods. This is a mistake for several reasons.

Foods provide a well-rounded nutrient combination. Any food choice will provide a combination of nutrients. For example, broccoli is known as a good source of vitamin C, and it also contains vitamin A and calcium. While milk is known mainly for its calcium content, it also contains vitamins A and D. The individual who takes a calcium supplement, instead of eating broccoli or drinking milk, misses out on vitamins A, C, and D in the process.

Not one food is a perfect food: While foods may contain nutrient combinations, no one food is nutritionally complete. Broccoli has a high vitamin and mineral content, yet it is not a good source of riboflavin or thiamin. Milk is an excellent riboflavin source, yet it lacks vitamin C. Eating a wide variety of food ensures that necessary nutrients are obtained in adequate amounts.

Supplements do not provide energy: Vitamins and minerals do not provide energy; they simply help metabolize calories into energy. Carbohydrates, proteins, fats, vitamins and minerals must be eaten in order to produce energy for working muscles. As previously described, we must consume carbohydrates, proteins, and fats in certain proportions. These ratios promote optimal energy availability.

How to Get Your Nutrients

Nutrients are commonly found in the food they metabolize. Vitamin E is known for its antioxidant properties. Good sources of vitamin E are polyunsaturated oils, which would be oxidized to rancidity without vitamin E. This is nature's way of ensuring that the calories and nutrients are available in the proper proportions at the right time. Consuming large amounts of nutrients without consuming the foods which they metabolize is a waste of time and money.

The National Dairy Council developed the 'Basic Four' concept to provide a blueprint for obtaining a variety of foods in adequate combinations. The brochure describing this method is a practical guideline for choosing a healthy combination of nutrients. Remember that there are high- and low-fat items in each of the four food categories. Choosing low-fat items instead of high-fat ones will help you achieve a high carbohydrate/low fat intake, which promotes the highest energy levels.

Fluids

Fluids, in the form of water, are essential for proper functioning of the body. The weight of the human body is 60—70 % water. A loss of 2—3% of this total can have serious results. Water provides a means for calorie and nutrient distribution. During exercise, muscles can produce 200 times the heat that muscles at rest do. Sweat provides a cooling function.

An important fact to remember about water is that its replenishment is a preventive strategy. The human thirst reflex is not sensitive enough to signal the early stages of dehydration. Therefore, by the time most individuals are thirsty, their fluid stores have been depleted past the point where they can be quickly replaced. Drink water before you notice that you need it.

General guidelines for fluid maintenance can be stated as follows:

☐ Drink 10—20 ounces of water up to 30 minutes prior

Know how much your bottle holds to make sure you have enough water for a ride.

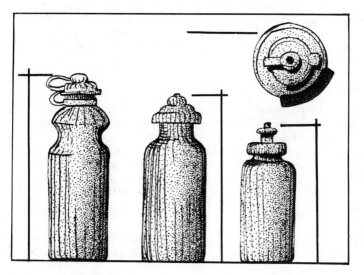

The concentration of electrolytes and carbohydrates in a sports drink should not exceed 7% of the mixed solution.

to riding.

☐ Drink an additional 8—12 ounces every 15—20 minutes while riding.

☐ At the end of a ride, replenish with 10—20 ounces of water.

Use a measuring cup to determine how many ounces your favorite cup and water bottle hold.

If possible, weigh yourself before and after your outing. For every pound lost, drink 16 ounces of water. Boost your fluid intake by eating foods with a high water content. Foods that are liquid at room temperature or contain liquid at room temperature are suitable, i.e fruits, vegetables, soups, jello, and pudding. Avoid beverages that contain caffeine and alcohol. Those two items appear in sodas, coffee, tea, chocolate, beer, wine, and hard liquor. They are diuretics, meaning they promote fluid loss.

Sports Drinks

Sport drinks are a widely available and heavily-marketed fluid choice. Their advertised benefit is that they contribute electrolytes (sodium and potassium) and provide carbohydrate energy. This implies an increased riding endurance. Does that mean you should add these items to your fluid intake? It depends on your individual situation. Perspiration, which every cyclist produces, does contain electrolytes. Research has shown conditioning decreases the amount of electrolytes lost with perspiration. Additionally, most people get more than an adequate supply of sodium and potassium in their regular diet. Therefore the benefits of further supplementation with a sports drink are questionable.

The amount of available carbohydrate is a factor that

limits cycling endurance. Yet carbohydrate stores are not normally depleted until two hours into a prolonged riding session. For an afternoon jaunt, it may not be necessary to consume a carbohydrate concentrate. Too high a concentration of additives may cause delivery to needy tissue to be delayed.

Studies have shown that as long as the solution concentration does not exceed 7%, fluid absorption will not be slowed down. It is important to check the manufacturer's specifications for the proper dilution instructions for sports drinks.

Timing Your Intake

A well-balanced diet is only part of the picture. In order for muscles to work at their strongest, most efficient levels, they must receive the proper amount of food at the right time. You wouldn't pour gasoline on your car engine and expect it to be well utilized, would you? Your automobile and your body need systems that distribute fuel at the right time, at the right rate. While your body doesn't have a carburetor or fuel injection system to perform this function, you can optimize your fuel distribution by timing your meals to match your activity, and to maintain the proper balance of 'carbs' to fat.

Basic Strategies

Remember to have a full energy supply at the beginning of a session. The most obvious way to implement this is to eat at regular intervals. Skipping meals depletes glycogen stores, which decreases available energy.

Individuals who skip meals often make the calorie deficit up at some point with one large high-fat meal, eating more calories than can be immediately metabolized. These calories go into cold fat storage rather than being converted into glycogen. While fat stores are plentiful in most individuals, glycogen stores must be regularly filled. Skipping meals can sabotage your nervous system and cycling coordination (as well as your muscular endurance) by storing fuel in a place where it is least needed. Your central nervous system and muscles keep the glucose they need to perform. Therefore adequate carbohydrates must be eaten at regular intervals to maintain essential glycogen stores.

Eating a high-carbohydrate meals is commonly called 'carbohydrate loading,' 'carbo-loading' or simply 'loading.' True carbohydrate-loading is a ritual (performed mainly by marathon athletes whose body's glycogen stores are depleted over a period of days with a combination of heavy exercise and low carbohydrate dieting. This depletion phase is followed by a low-exercise, extremely high-carbo-hydrate diet, which overloads glycogen stores and provides a larger store of carbohydrates from which to draw during extended exercise sessions. This type of carbo-loading has several side effects, including weight gain and irritability, and is hard on the liver. Therefore it should not be ex-ecuted frequently and is recommended only for rare events such as marathons. No such ritual is necessary for a typi-cal mountain biker. If you eat a lot of carbohydrates a lot of the time, you will maintain your glycogen stores at an adequate level.

Another important point that is often overlooked is replet-ing energy stores after a ride. Most people think of carbo-hydrate loading as a pre-cycling activity. Yet if carbo-load-ing is not complemented by post-cycling hydrocarbon in-take as well, glycogen stores are not maintained at their optimum levels. This is an especially important concept for individuals who ride at least more than once a day. Eating something like a large bowl of lentil soup and some cornbread after a heavy bike outing is as important as eating a large spaghetti dinner the night before. It replaces the energy which has just been used and ensures that the next day of cycling will be just as enjoyable as the last one.

A popular misconception among athletes is that beer is a good carbohydrate food. This is really wishful thinking, as one beer has only about as many carbohydrate calories as a slice of bread. About 63% of the calories in a regular beer are alcohol calories, which are metabolized more like fat than carbohydrate.

Meal Planning

The strategies discussed so far can be taken one step fur-ther: Tailor your eating patterns to match the activity pat-terns you prefer. You can optimize the amount and type of fuel you need when it is most needed. Look at your biking schedule. Are you riding early in the morning or before breakfast? Do you jam the pedals in the late afternoon, perhaps after a hard day at work?

Now look at your eating pattern. Does your intake cor-respond to your activity? Or are you riding hard in the morning and eating most of your calories in the evening? You may need to adjust your eating so it matches your ac-tivity pattern. The following guidelines are provided for the most common schedules; you may need to adjust your own eating to meet your own unique itinerary.

It can be a lot of fun to wake up at 4 in the morning to eat in time for a 7 AM ride....

Morning Rides

Training first thing in the morning presents several challenges. Your performance is best if you have eaten a few hours before the activity. It is recommended that meals not be consumed within 2—3 hours prior to a prolonged activity, a morning rider would have to rise a 3 or 4 a.m., eat, and then wait in the dark for two hours before getting on the bike. You may enjoy the solitude, but other options do exist.

For those who prefer to eat most of their breakfast before exercising, eating a breakfast that is mostly liquid at least one hour before training is the recommended plan of action. Liquids move through the digestive tract faster than solids, so they can be consumed with less lead time. Examples of liquid (or mostly liquid) breakfasts include the following:

☐ Lots of water, juice and toast.

☐ 8 ounces of skim milk and a piece of toast.

☐ 8 ounces of skim milk with cereal.

☐ 4 ounces of yogurt mixed with grapenuts, raisins and honey.

☐ a carton of nonfat yogurt.

☐ a yogurt smoothie.

Note that the liquid in most of these cases is a dairy product. These foods provide complex rather than simple carbohydrates, and also supply protein. Protein extends energy levels for a long exercise session. Choosing cereals and yogurt without large amounts of added sugar will also help minimize the simple carbohydrate content of these meals. For those who want to limit dairy intake, here are two different recipes for a good early morning meal.

Scrambled Tofu

3	tablespoons oil
1/4	teaspoon cumin
1	tablespoon instant mixed onion or 1/2 cup sauteed onions
1/4	teaspoon poultry seasoning
2	cups tofu
1	tablespoon soy sauce

Put in skillet and mix until seasonings are distributed. Serve like scrambled eggs. Try it wrapped in a tortilla.

Peanut Butter Paté

1/2	lb. tofu, drained
1/2	cup smooth peanut butter
1	tablespoon lemon juice
1	teaspoon lemon rind, grated
2	tablespoons honey

Blend together or puree in food processor. Spread on rice cakes, english muffins, etc. Keeps in refrigerator several days.

If you cannot face food the first thing in the morning, here is an alternative: consume a small amount of carbohydrates immediately before cycling, and maintain glucose levels by consuming small amounts of carbohydrate at regular intervals (every thirty minutes) throughout the ride. A good initial choice would be a dairy product. Some type of fruit juice (diluted to half strength to promote hydration) would be acceptable as well.

Consuming food during a ride is optional. Popular portable choices include bananas, orange slices, fig bars, raisins, and dried fruit. Some riders even report enjoying baked potatoes while out on the trail.

Avoid eating anything in the 30—60 minutes before exercising, because blood would be shunted from would-be exercising muscles to the digestive tract, so the blood and energy supply to the muscles and nervous system is decreased.

Afternoon Rides

Afternoon or pre-dinner training is common. Eat a large breakfast and a medium-sized lunch for afternoon and early evening rides. This will ensure that enough energy has been consumed to support the early day's activities. It will also stock muscle glycogen stores with energy for the late afternoon ride. Lunch can be timed to be eaten 2—3 hours before riding. A small snack can be added in the early afternoon.

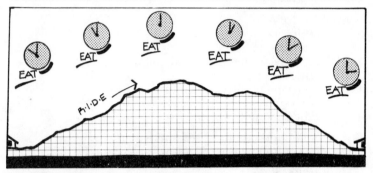

Eat small amounts of food every hour to maintain a constant flow of energy to muscles and brain.

A common side effect of activity is a decrease in appetite. You may not feel like eating after a vigorous ride. Remember, restocking your glycogen stores after your workout is important. If you can manage to eat some complex carbohydrates within an hour after the ride, glycogen replenishment will be optimized. If you don't enjoy working in the kitchen after a long ride, prepare a batch of lasagna, split pea soup, or pasta salad ahead of time, so that it is ready when you return from your workout.

Evening Rides

Just as with afternoon rides, it is important to eat a light meal well before the ride. If dinner and riding are within 2—3 hours of each other, be sure to add liquids (in the form of soup, beverages, and/or yogurt) to the menu. Again remember to eat a snack after the ride for glycogen replenishment — examples include half a bagel with peanut butter, half a sandwich, pasta salad, yogurt smoothie, fruit, and skim milk.

If you enjoy a traditional meal, another option would be to split the large meal into two smaller servings, eating the items with higher fat content upon returning from the ride.

All-day Outings

In the case of an all-day trip, it is best to eat small, frequent snacks throughout. That is called 'grazing.' Constant eating provides a constant supply of energy without overloading the digestive tract or overstimulating insulin. A good rule of thumb is that every third or fourth fluid stop should also be a snack break. Avoid eating a large lunch midway through the day. This action may promote sluggishness, decreasing concentration and endurance. Again, rejuvenate your glycogen stores with a carbohydrate feast when the day is over.

The food you eat greatly influences your cycling performance and enjoyment. This detailed information may suggest that good nutrition requires hours of planning and
preparation. That's not true: A healthy diet for any sport
only requires remembering a few simple rules:

☐ Eat foods that are high in complex carbohydrates, and
  low in simple carbohydrates and fat.

☐ Eat a variety of foods.

☐ Drink as much fluid as you can remember to.

☐ Coordinate your eating with your activity.

You will find that just a few minutes of planning each day
can greatly improve your dietary repertoire, which, in
turn, can lead to better biking.

Chapter 6
Health and Safety
_____ in the Outdoors

This chapter and those that follow will provide guidelines you can use to help ensure that your time in the wilderness is not only safe for you, but for others and for the environment as well. Being efficient and competent outside has many rewards. Two of the biggies are an increase in independent fun, and a maximum margin of safety.

When engaging in any kind of activity outside, it helps to set priorities. Obviously, safety is of utmost importance, and takes precedence over personal goals and trip objectives. But safety for whom? Outdoors you always need to consider your own safety, as well as the safety of others, of the environment, and the safety of your equipment. As a mountain biker and as members of a technical society, you are equipment-dependent. Taking care of that equipment increases our ability to take care of yourselves and others.

In personal terms, however, your equipment is not as important as the environment, nor is the environment as important as the health of you or other members of your party. For instance, you should not ride hell-bent down a mountain tundra slope just to reach biking euphoria, but you may have to cut down a small tree if that's what it takes to make a splint for a broken leg.

With this priority scheme in mind, let's get down to the nitty gritty of how to meet nature and enjoy what it has to offer us, with that enjoyment based on good judgment and ecological integrity.

Time Control Plans

A Time Control Plans, or TCP, is an invaluable component of safety when heading out on an excursion, whether it be a fifty-mile bike ride down the road to the next town or a multi-day backcountry expedition in your favorite national forest. It is something to implement before you even crank the gears and hit the trail, and it can be modified according to your needs.

A TCP is used in part as an itinerary. Leave it with someone on the home front who is responsible and who can handle an emergency situation, someone whom you trust and whose trust has been substantiated through past experience.

A complete TCP, for example one which would be used for a week-long desert canyon trip, should include the following:

1. Date

2. Leader's name

3. Names of group members

4. List of group gear (including amount of food being taken)

5. Map names

6. Origin (where you are leaving from)

7. Destination (where you are going) — detailed route description:
    a. mileage
    b. points of reference
    c. specific landforms

8. Linear Distance (LD)

9. Total Elevation Gain (TEG) — cumulative (count all elevation gain — do not count elevation lost in between)

10. Adjusted Mileage (mileage from Point 8 plus one mile for each 1000 ft gained per Point 9)

11. Estimated Time of Departure/Estimated Time of Arrival (ETD/ETA)

12. Rate of travel considerations: elevation gain, obstacles, group strength, weather, rest breaks, and whatever else you can think of that influences progress.

13. Total Travel Time (TTT) — can be used instead of, or in addition to, ETD/ETA

Obviously, a TCP as complete as the one described above is not needed for every bike trip you take. It has many advantages, however, and the more serious you become about taking challenging trips into the wilds, the more complete you will want it to be.

Look at it from two angles. As a competent outdoors enthusiast, it gives you some helpful information. What kind of terrain and topography are you going to be encountering on this trip? A TCP forces you to look closely at your topographic maps. What kind of capabilities is your group going to need in order to manage this awe-inspiring trip? Do all the participants have those capabilities? Remember, skills need to be there, along with ambition, before you enter the backcountry. You want your trip to be fun and

challenging, not harrowing. Do you have all the gear necessary to meet the unexpected? If you don't, chances are you
will need it — and there's nothing worse than knowing it is
back home in the closet and you just overlooked bringing
it.

Now look at TCP's from an other angle, the angle of your
brother or close friend whom you have told your expedition would be home by Monday morning, noon at the
latest, and it is now late Monday evening. A thorough TCP
left in good hands is going to provide the right people with
the right information. They know who is gone and what
equipment the missing party has to care of themselves.
They know from where they left, where they're going, and
which route they're taking. All that's critically important
information if a search party has to be sent out, or if an
evacuation needs to take place.

The time taken to put together a good TCP is well worth
the effort. Practice writing them, either individually or with
the group you are going with. When it comes time to actually use one, make two copies; one is for you to refer to
on your trip, while the other is for your outside contact.
Whatever you do, don't leave this kind of information in
your car. Sometimes people do this as a precaution in
case they don't return within a reasonable time. Not only
does this leave your well-being in the dubious hands of
strangers, with the off-chance that they will find it in time,
but it also invites vandalism. It is a sad ending to a suc-
cessful trip to come back and find that others have broken
into your vehicle.

Safety in Numbers vs. Going it Alone

It is a wonderful experience to head into the backcountry
in the quiet solitude a solo trip offers, whether it be for a
day, a long weekend, or for a two-week hiatus. Peace of
mind, spiritual and personal growth, and intimacy with nature are all aspects of a solitary journey that are not as
easily attained when accompanied by others.

As with any good thing, however, some considerations involved with a solo trip come to mind that make traveling
with some friends a very attractive alternative. Obviously,
the main issue here, again, is *safety*, especially in an isolated or backcountry environment.

The great advantage of biking with at least three other
people is that in a serious situation, responsibilities can
be delegated and carried out with efficiency. The worst-
case scenario is that someone in the party gets hurt to the
extent that outside help is needed. Remember, it is the

worst-case scenario that you must think about and
prepare for before leaving the house. In a group of four,
that leaves one person to administer first-aid and monitor
the patient, while the other two people go for help. This
would be the ideal situation.

Somebody who is hurt should never be left alone; it could
be devastating for his or her psychological and physical
condition. It is a scary thing to be hurt and to be left in
the outdoors, and that kind of stress can lead to irrational
behavior and/or a worsening physical condition. You also
want to prevent bikers from having to travel by themselves, especially in an emergency, and so the two people
should preferably go together to obtain help. This reduces
the tendency to rush and get hurt or lost.

First-Aid Training

As you spend more time on the bike, and as you become
more skilled with it, you may find that more enticing and
challenging rides are beckoning you. You may be at that
point now. Good! Get on with it, but do it sensibly. Be
serious about your sport, with as many factors on your
side as possible. That means knowing as much first-aid as
possible. Take a first-responder course, or one in advanced first-aid. Better yet, work on getting your emergency medical technician (EMT) certificate. There are some excellent wilderness EMT (W-EMT) courses available in
many parts of the country which are specifically geared
towards first-aid improvisation and backcountry care. At
the very least become certified yearly in cardiopulmonary
resuscitation (CPR). Here are four good sources of wilderness first aid training:

☐ SOLO, RFD 1, Box 163, Conway, NH 03818, Tel.: (603)
447-6711

☐ NASAR Wilderness Medicine, RFD 2, Box 890, Bryant
Pond, ME 04219, Tel.: (207) 665-2707

☐ Wilderness First Aid and Safety Association of British
Columbia, c/o Outdoor Recreation Department,
Capilano College, 2055 Purcell Way North, Vancouver
BC V75 3H5, Canada

☐ Kurt Hahn Center, c/o North Carolina Outward Bound
School, 121 North Sterling Street, Morganton, NC
28655-3443 (prerequisite: Basic EMT)

In addition to these four programs, there are many others.

Check your surrounding area. With these qualifications, the backcountry opens up to you, and you are more ready to meet with its challenges and its splendor. A solo trip, or a trip with fewer than four members, becomes a safer bet. You are a more valuable member to any mountain biking expedition, whether it be in a wilderness setting or on your home town's streets and bike trails.

Medical Emergencies

Odds are that the more time you spend in athletic activities outdoors, the greater chance you have of encountering a situation where outside assistance is required. In such cases, it is important to be calm, and in as much control of the situation (and yourself!) as possible.

Stop. Breathe deeply. Think clearly. Take the time necessary to organize; know what needs to be done, and know how those needs are going to be met before you act.

Hopefully, you or someone in your party will have had training in first aid and emergency procedures. If you haven't, but someone else has, listen to him or her. Do what is asked of you and pay attention. Only perform first-aid to the level of your ability and training. At the very least, know what information to carry out with you if you need to get help. Be sure the information is written down; don't entrust the health and care of another to your memory, especially in what could be intimidating circumstances.

Here is a list of the pieces of information you should attempt to gather and carry out with you. It is in the format of a SOAP note, which is what many ambulance crews and rescue personnel use in one form or another. SOAP stands for the initials of the four categories of information contained: Subjective, Objective, Assesment and Plan.

SOAP Note

S — Subjective
Age, sex, the chief complaint the patient has (in his or her own words as much as possible), and the mechanism of injury (MOI).

O — Objective
Patient exam: describe the location of pain and what the injuries are.

Vital Signs: time, respiration rate, pulse, skin, temperature, consciousness/mental status (C/MS), blood pressure.

History: A: allergies, M: medications, P: past history (previous injury or illness), L: last meal, E: events (leading up to the accident).

A — Assessment
Problem list: developed from information in S and O above
(e.g., vomiting, shortness of breath, swollen right ankle).
The specificity of this problem list depends on your level of
training, experience and diagnostic tools.

P — Plan
Develop a treatment plan from the problem list above. For
multiple problems, have complete treatment plans for
each problem incorporated into one plan of action. The
last plan is to monitor the patient as often as circumstances dictate. Keep him or her sheltered from the environment, and realize that injuries augment the patient's sus-
ceptibility to environmental factors. Anticipate future problems the patient may have, and be ready to change your
problem list and treatment as necessary.

Not all this information will be attainable all of the time,
but strive to collect what you can. When someone is unconscious, look for medical-alert tags around his or her
neck or wrist. The patient may have a special condition
(diabetes, epilepsy, etc.) that aggravates the situation and
potential rescuers need to know about. *Never* move someone whom you suspect has neck or back injuries, unless
his or her life is in immediate danger from environmental
causes (rockfall, running water, etc.) or unless you are
qualified to do so. If the need does arise, do it with as little
movement of their head and spinal cord as possible.

It is a good idea to always carry pen and paper with you in
case you need it in circumstances like these. You could
even carry a blank SOAP note to use immediately when
you need it. A sample is on the next page.

Again, get as much training as you can in first aid. It is
cheap insurance, not only for yourself but for the friends
and family with whom you play hard.

Environmental Injuries

Besides obvious bleeding from a traumatic injury,
hypothermia and heat stroke are two of the few true outdoor emergencies requiring immediate and specific attention to prevent death. I want to mention them briefly so
you can take preventive measures. Prevention is the key:
these emergencies are easy to avoid and the consequences
of not doing so are rapid and devastating.

Hypothermia;

Hypothermia is one of the major causes of death for out-

SOAP Note

(no Copyright, this page only)

S — Subjective (age, sex, chief complaint, MOI)

_____
_____
_____
_____
_____

O — Objective (PE, VS, AMPLE) Physical exam: location of pain and injuries

_____
_____
_____
_____
_____

Vital Signs:
Time: _____
RR: _____
P: _____
Skin: _____
Temp.: _____
C/MS: _____
BP: _____

A: _____
M: _____
P: _____
L: _____
E: _____

A — Assessment (problem list)

_____
_____
_____
_____
_____

P — Plan (treatment plan, monitoring)

_____
_____
_____
_____
_____

door enthusiasts, mountain bikers included. A person becomes hypothermic when his or her body core temperature drops below 95°F, or 35°C. It does not need to be very cold for a person to become hypothermic: most cases occur when the ambient temperature is in the 60's. Although you may not know what a person's body temperature is at any given moment, there are preliminary signs and symptoms a person exhibits when becoming hypothermic (as described below), and everyone should be alert to them. When addressed immediately, the process is quickly reversed. If not, the patient will quickly succumb to the point where advanced hospital care will be required.

Prevention of Hypothermia

There are four general ways in which the body transfers, and therefore loses, heat to the environment.

Convection:
Your body creates a thin micro-environment of warm air that surrounds it and buffers you from the outside air temperature. Through wind and body movement, this layer is constantly being stripped away, and the body is continually losing heat as it attempts to maintain this protective barrier.

Conduction:
Conduction is the exchange of heat from one object to another. Whenever the body comes in contact with a colder object, conductive heat loss will occur.

Radiation:
Radiation is heat transferred by electromagnetic waves from one (warmer) object to another (colder) one. The body lose heat through the emission of infrared energy. Any area of the body with direct exposure to the environment will radiate heat. Because the head has a large blood supply that cannot be restricted, radiant heat loss from this area is the most significant. At 39°F, or 4°C, an uncovered head can lose up to 50% of the body's total heat production!

Evaporation:
Energy is required to change water from a liquid to a gas. Even though there is no temperature change, heat is absorbed; this is called the 'latent heat of evaporation'. Evaporative heat loss takes place when the body sweats or when wet clothes are drying on the body. The process itself absorbs the heat that the body loses.

In order to minimize heat loss, simple precautionary

sures can be taken.

☐ Wear protective clothing that insulates and protects against wind and moisture. Proper clothing will be discussed in the next chapter.

☐ Cover your head with a helmet or a hat.

☐ Decrease the surface contact your body has with cold surfaces. For example, while taking a rest break from a good hard ride, don't stretch out on the ground. Instead, rest sitting up on something that insulates you from the ground, keeping an air space between you and the ground.

In addition to minimizing any extraneous heat loss, you should be producing inner heat as efficiently as possible. Here are some guidelines to follow:

☐ Eat right, and eat enough. Heat is produced as a byproduct of cell metabolism, a prerequisite for life. The source of metabolic heat is energy from the carbohydrate, fat, and protein you munch down. Proper nutrition was discussed in the chapter 4.

☐ Drink lots of water. This cannot be emphasized enough. The body needs at least 1500 ml (1.6 qts.) a day to function properly, and this amount increases with exercise. During respiration, air must be warmed to body core temperature with humidity close to 100%. When biking in cold and dry conditions, the amount of moisture lost through respiration is significant, and must be replenished. By the time you experience thirst, you are already behind in your water intake. In order to keep up with this loss, drink fair amounts of water, at frequent intervals. If you don't have a couple of water bottle cages on your bike, or behind your saddle, put them on. The more accessible your water, the more likely you will drink it regularly. Besides taking care of other ailments, proper water consumption reduces a body's potential for aggravated heat loss. Studies have shown that experiencing 10% dehydration causes a 30—40% decrease in thermal control (*Hypothermia Death by Exposure*, William W. Forgey M.D., 1985, p. 29).

☐ Exercise is not too much of a problem for mountain bikers, but there are a few relevant facts to remember about volitional exercise. Along with basal metabolism, skeletal muscle activity generates a significant amount of body heat. The more conditioned you are physically, the easier it is for the body to adapt to cold stress. Being fit will also reduce the likelihood that prolonged

exercise will exhaust you. Exhaustion can quickly lead to hypothermia. If the body is so tired that muscular activity cannot take place, the muscle's energy substrate glycogen has been completely consumed. Physical conditioning augments the body's ability to replace and utilize more efficiently muscle glycogen.

When going for bike rides, keep this information in mind. When you take rest breaks, eat some food, drink some water, put on another layer of clothing, and make sure you are minimizing any heat loss from convection, conduction, radiation, and evaporation. When you begin to feel chilled, get back on the bike and start pedaling again. Remember that the environment can seem deceptively benign, and it only takes some unpreparedness — and/or a lackadaisical attitude — to get yourself or someone else into a serious medical emergency, even on a sunny and warm day. If a person does begin to show signs of cold stress, he or she may exhibit all or some of the following:

1. Discomfort — a sensation of feeling cold.

2. Cold diuresis — the tendency to urinate more often than usual. The body has started to shut down normal blood circulation to the extremities in order to keep the body core warm, and will therefore need to get rid of the 'extra' fluid volume it is now carrying.

3. Skin discoloration — the skin may become somewhat pale and cool. Cyanosis, a characteristic bluish color, may be seen around the lips and fingernails.

4. Mild shivering — shivering, being an uncontrollable rhythmic contraction and relaxation of skeletal muscle, is an emergency method the body uses to generate heat.

5. Sometimes loss of dexterity.

6. Consciousness and mental state of the patient is normal.

If the body is unable to produce more heat than he or she is losing, the patient will enter into mild to moderate hypothermia, as the body's compensatory mechanisms begin to be overwhelmed. The signs and symptoms will include the following:

1. Cold discomfort may be extreme.

2. Cold diuresis continues.

3. The skin will continue to exhibit signs of cyanosis where mucous membranes are present, and will be pale and cool in other areas.

4. Shivering will be mild to severe.

5. Dexterity may be severely reduced from shivering and loss of peripheral nerve function.

6. Consciousness and mental state will exhibit mild to moderate alterations, with a person's higher thinking functions becoming impaired, along with personality changes. They may become irritable, lethargic, apathetic, and/or withdrawn. They lose their ability to problem-solve and make sound judgment decisions. The patient's mental state is your biggest clue that something is amiss.

7. Core body temperature ranges between 90°F and 98.6° F (32.2°C and 37.0°C, respectively).

At this point, aggressive action needs to be taken if the hypothermic process is to be reversed. Remember, even in mild to moderate hypothermia, the victim loses the ability to correctly assess the situation and therefore the ability to help him or herself. Treatment by others must be quick and efficient, and relevant to the circumstances.

☐ Shelter the patient from environmental forces contributing to the problem: wind, rain, cold.

☐ Insulate the patient with warm and dry clothing. Make sure the face and head are insulated.

☐ Give him or her food and water. Any liquids given should be warm — neither hot nor cold. Hot liquid will vasodilate the extremities and subsequently cool the body core. Never give alcohol or coffee to someone who is hypothermic: both are diuretics and alcohol is a powerful vasodilator.

☐ Exercise the patient as appropriate under the circumstances. This requires caloric intake, of course.

If all the adequate measures have been taken, recovery at this point will be rapid and complete. Beyond this point, the person will slide into severe hypothermia; the signs, symptoms, and treatment will not be covered in this book: a person in severe hypothermia, is in desperate need of hospital care. Courses in outdoor emergency first aid cover hypothermia in its entirety, with much more information than can be given here. If you are prepared, aware of environmental conditions, and if you are keeping tabs on yourself and others, you should never see more than a mild stress response to the cold.

Heat Stroke

Heat stroke occurs when the body's internal mechanisms

for heat release fail, and core temperature then rises uncontrollably. Immediate action must be taken to halt and reverse this process. Death, or permanent residual disability are the common outcomes of untreated heat stroke.

The most likely reason heat stroke might overtake a mountain biker is prolonged exercise in a hot and humid clime, especially if the rider is experiencing any sort of fluid or salt depletion. Young athletic people are actually more prone to heat stroke than many others. Here are the signs and symptoms of heat stroke — their onset is very rapid:

1. Any sort of change in mental state or function: irrational behavior and confusion are common, often followed by disorientation, uncontrollable anxiety, uncoordination, delirium, and unconsciousness. As in hypothermia, the patient's mental state is your biggest clue that there is a problem.

2. Convulsions are common.

3. Pupils of the eyes may be dilated and unresponsive to light.

4. The skin feels hot to the touch, and may either be wet from perspiration or dry because the body can no longer compensate through sweating mechanisms.

5. Pulse is high.

6. Respiratory rate is high.

7. Shock is usually present.

Treatment of heat stroke is as follows:

Evacuate a heat stroke victim to medical help as soon as possible

☐ Act quickly: any delay increases the patient's chance of irreversible residual disability.

☐ If the patient becomes unconscious, maintain an open airway.

☐ If appropriate, treat for shock; elevate the legs.

☐ Make sure the patient is out of direct sunlight and in as cool and shady a place as possible.

Use any method feasible to cool the victim down quickly. Clothing should be removed and the skin fanned to increase heat loss through evaporation and convection. If available, cool, wet towels or clothing can be placed on the trunk and extremities.

While cooling the patient down, massage his or her extremities vigorously to aid the flow of cooled blood back into the organs and the head.

Ice packs or ice cold water will vasoconstrict the extremities, actually delaying the efficiency of the cooling process and can causing cold injuries. Cool water is therefore preferable.

☐ Once you have brought the person's temperature down sufficiently (assessed through mental state, pulse, respiration rate), immediately start monitoring his or her condition closely to prevent the body's temperature from rising unexpectedly again. It is also common for a person's temperature to rebound three to four hours after cooling. If you continue to actively cool the patient past the point where such aggressive means are no longer necessary, the he or she could go into hypothermia.

☐ Evacuate the patient to a hospital as soon as possible. This is especially important if unconsciousness has occurred, but professional medical help should be sought regardless. The list of possible heat stroke complications is lengthy and serious: liver failure, kidney failure, blood clotting abnormalities, biochemical alterations, gastrointestinal ulceration accompanied by bleeding, heart damage, and extensive brain damage.

Not fun, but again, prevention is the answer. Monitor your body comfort, and stay on top of it. Do what you need to do to keep it under control. That usually means adding and shedding layers of clothes constantly; a 24-hour job, but well worth it.

Chapter 7

Clothing for
Off-Road Cycling

There was a time when deciding what to wear for an outdoor activity was relatively easy, but in these days of high-tech, the task can seem daunting. Everywhere people seem to be wearing the latest miracle cloth in the latest colors, with an attached tag guaranteeing better performance. Just separating product names from brand names can be difficult. Fortunately, the reasons why we wear what we do wear have not changed, and understanding these concepts will allow you to make the right choices for the type of riding you do, keeping you comfortable and safe.

With biking, as with any other active outdoor sport, the key to clothing selection is function. Clothes should allow for comfort and efficiency. Physical activity generates a lot of body heat, which the body tries to dissipate through perspiration. In warm weather, you want this heat to be lost; in colder weather this heat needs to be retained.

When air contacts the skin, convection occurs, and the heat brought to the skin's surface by perspiration is transferred to the surrounding air. In hot, dry weather, this is exactly what you want to happen, and riding augments the process. Cotton is wonderful in such a situation, be-

The body maintains a micro-climate around its surface. The blowing wind or physical movement disturbs this layer. Consequently, the body expends more energy in maintaining this micro-climate. Dress in layers to be able to adjust to temperature changes, and use a wind-resistant outer layer when it is cold.

cause its fibers hold and absorb sweat; air passes through the cloth and cools the skin. The more voluminous and light the cotton is, and the more loosely it is worn, the better it will allow for the cooling of the skin.

In colder weather, you want to trap the warmth your body produces with insulating air pockets, stay as dry as possible, and maintain a comfortable temperature regardless of weather conditions or level of activity. This is best achieved by dressing in layers. There are three basic components to the layering system: the inner layer, the insulating layer, and the protective layer. Each layer has a different function in controlling your body comfort.

1. *Inner layer* (underwear): Being closest to your skin, it should carry moisture away from your body for either evaporation or transportation to the next clothing layer.

2. *Insulation layer:* This is the thermal layer where the majority of warmth is retained. There are many new synthetic insulators on the market, which we will discuss later. Wool has always been the standard insulator because it works well even when wet, even though it was around long before any of the synthetics.

3. *Protective Layer:* This is the outer layer that should be designed to keep rain or wind from penetrating into the other two layers. The outer garment must be either waterproof or water repellent. Whereas water repellent fabrics are breathable, allowing for some air exchange, waterproof fabrics do not allow for air exchange.

While we're talking about outerwear, let's talk about raingear, and one person's personal philosophy about riding in the rain: It is fantastic! Do it, but expect to get wet. There are many products out there that are claimed to be waterproof and breathable. In a few years we may actually have a material that can do both things at once, but for the present we can't yet have our cake and eat it, too. Gore-Tex, Sympatex, VersaTech, and other similar laminate/weave products work as well as they can, but they are hardly water repellent, much less waterproof in an aggressive rain. In a good downpour, the moisture is either going to come from sweating or from the rain.

If you wear bomber raingear while exercising even halfway vigorously, it cannot and will not breathe, and you will be saturated with your own perspiration. If you wear a supposedly 'waterproof yet breathable' rain shell in anything but a light mist, you will get wet from the outside in. In order to work as well as possible, garments made with these fabrics must be kept very clean, and that is often unrealistic. I find the most comfortable way is to wear an insulating layer with a wind shell. I'll be wet, but I'll be warm without suffocating in my trapped body heat, and I'll dry out rather quickly when conditions permit.

Instead of fabric weaves, some companies use fabric treatments to keep rain and mist on the outside. Helly-Tech is a microporous polyurethane treatment that Helly-Hanson combines with Supplex nylon. Ultrex is basically the same thing, put out by Burlington Mills. DuPont puts out an oil and water repellent spray called Zepel, which you can reapply yourself, and which DuPont uses in the manufacturing process. All of these products work to a degree; my personal belief is that a good insulating layer with a windbreaker is simpler and just as effective.

I only mention these different products because they are popular and you will run into their names when looking for gear. Nowhere am I advocating any one brand over another. And in describing natural and synthetic fibers, what they are and where they come from, you will have some background information when shopping. First we'll discuss natural fibers, then the synthetics.

Cotton

Most people agree that cotton is one of the most comfortable fabrics around, which accounts for its wide popularity. Cotton is a durable, cellulosic fiber harvested from the cotton plant seed. The fibers are very short, ½ to 2½ inches long, and are hydrophilic: they absorb and retain moisture easily. On a hot summer day, when no rain has been seen for weeks and you are going for a quick 60 minute bike ride, cotton is a fine thing to wear. Let the weather change suddenly, however, and get that favorite T-shirt and pair of shorts wet, and they instantly turn into death cloth next to your skin. Through èconduction, cotton will drain your body of its warmth while at the same time refusing to dry. Whatever insulating properties it had when dry, and they are negligible to begin with, are now completely defunct. It would be best not to be wearing it at all, at this point. For this reason, you should be very careful about wearing cotton in any situation where your safety and warmth might be at risk.

Wool

Wool is an amazing natural insulator. The natural crimp of its fibers traps the surrounding air, providing a microclimate of warmth surrounding your body. Wool fibers range in length from one to 18 inches, and therefore can be used to make many types of garments with differing qualities.

Quality wool clothing often still contains the natural oil, or yolk, of the fibers. Yolk consists of wool grease and suet, or dried sheep perspiration. Some wools can therefore tend towards being hydrophobic, repelling water fairly well. On the whole, however, wool does absorb water. The fibers do not compact when wet, though, so they maintain those air pockets that help retain body heat. Wool would be an excellent medium to use for your insulating layer. It is affordable, works in adverse weather conditions, and is a natural way to use less petroleum-based synthetics. Some of the disadvantages of wool are that it is both heavier and more bulky than today's high-tech insulators. Other natural fibers that insulate well are alpaca, mohair, vicuna, and cashmere.

Linen

Linen is a smooth, strong fabric made from the stem of the flax plant. It absorbs moisture and dries quickly. Its fiber range between six and 20 inches in length. A lot of casual outdoor wear is made from a blend of cotton and linen. As with cotton, linen is fine for a spin around town, but it does not insulate well — whether wet or dry.

Silk

This queen of fibers comes from the completed cocoon of the silkworm. It is the only natural filament fiber, its average length being 1000 to 1300 yards (or one cocoon's worth). To construct a cocoon, two streams of liquid silk pour out of glands near the silkworm's jaw while swinging its head from side to side in a figure-eight movement. The silk hardens on contact with the air.

Besides being elegantly beautiful, silk is the strongest natural fiber, stronger than a wire of the same diameter for many types of steel. It is fairly elastic, weighs very little, and is warmer than cotton, rayon, or linen. It therefore makes a good insulating underwear for moderate conditions. The disadvantage of silk is that it is not hydrophobic, retaining moisture and sweat instead of wicking it away from the skin as readily as synthetics.

Synthetics

Most active outdoor wear is now made of synthetics. To produce synthetic fibers, two or more elements are chemically combined to make a new compound. These polymers start as liquids that are pushed through tiny, fiber-width holes in spinnerets. The liquid fibers then harden, with their diameter, shape and density dependent upon the polymer composition and the spinneret used. Moisture transport, insulation, and heat dissipation can now be isolated and defined qualitatively to create use-specific fibers for almost any need. This technology has led to a variety of new synthetics, with new brand names introduced every year.

Rayon

Rayon fibers are made from natural cellulosic material — wood pulp or cotton linters — that have been chemically regenerated. Rayon was the first artificial fiber made, and is used in combination with other synthetics in many types of outdoor gear. It is a soft and versatile fiber that is hydrophobic (like most other synthetic fibers). Garments made with rayon make a good secondary insulation layer.

Nylon

Nylon is a lightweight, extremely strong and durable fiber made from chemicals found in coal, air, water, petroleum, natural gas or agricultural byproducts. It is now produced in many different forms, although it first appeared as women's hosiery in 1937. Nylon is abrasion resistant and is an excellent source for the third, or outer layer of clothing. Coated nylon is waterproof, and uncoated nylon acts as a good windbreaker. Compared to other synthetics, nylon is not very expensive.

Acrylic

In addition to being made out of mostly the same chemicals as nylon: coal, air, petroleum, while chemicals found in limestone are also used to make in acrylics. Articles made of this material are a good secondary insulating layer, being soft and warm, while absorbing very little moisture.

Spandex

Spandex, or Lycra, as DuPont calls the same material is a material with miniscule rubber bands in the weave that allow four-way stretch of the fabric. The world of fashion sportswear has definitely been taken over by the world of spandex. Biking shorts, shirts, helmet covers, riding gloves, and underwear are all being made of this material, or combinations of spandex with other fibers. In mild conditions, spandex clothing is a good choice. It is very comfortable, and its elasticity allows for active and unhindered movement. These fibers can be stretched over 500% and still return to their original length, without breaking.

Polyester

Polyester is the most widely used synthetic fiber in the world. Again, it is a derivative of water and coal or petroleum. Polyester clothes are hydrophobic .It can also be blended with natural fibers to create clothes with many different qualities. The majority of outdoor wear has some percentage of polyester in it. Cotton/polyester blends can work well in moderate conditions. They still allow for breathability, are less absorbent than all cotton, and dry quickly.

A popular brand-name made of polyester is Patagonia's Capilene, which virtually lasts forever. Capilene has been chemically designed to transport moisture. It also rids it-self more easily in the wash of perspiration oils and other types of dirt, a nice feature in the long haul.

Medalist makes a polyester/nylon fabric named Dryline, used in their Skinetics underwear, which is quite similar to Capilene. With a hydrophobic inner layer of polyester to transport moisture away from you, and absorbant nylon to pull that water from the outside, these garments are functional and easy to keep clean.

Another type of polyester is called pile. Pile, and retropile (pile turned inside out) wears fantastically well, being extremely durable and very warm. In the 'olden days,' pile used to pill up, forming little fuzz balls on the garment. Al-

It's entirely possible to ride in the rain — with the right clothing.

though this didn't hurt the function of the clothing at all, it wreaked havoc on the fashion-conscious. This has been rectified, with new types of pill-free pile on the market. Patagonia markets a pile called Synchilla. Malden Mills puts out a pile-like fleece under the names of PolarFleece, PolarLite, and PolarPlus.

Polypropylene

Used as underwear, polypropylene wicks moisture away from the skin very effectively. It was one of the first fabrics used in long underwear specifically for that reason. Along with being hydrophobic, it also has very good insulating qualities, and is very light. Over time, polypropylene loses its wicking abilities, and tends to retain perspiration odor to the nth degree because it is so hydrophobic — regardless of washing. Fabrics that are hydrophobic hate water, so they don't get along with the water in your washing machine either.

How to Dress Right

There are endless combinations of all the above. Dress in layers, so that you can easily adapt to changing weather conditions and changing levels of activity. If you become too warm, shed a layer; if too cold, add another layer to your system. Your clothes should protect you from the environment and from accidents. You may want to combine layers. For example, Bellwether makes shelled cycling tights called Ultima, which insulates and protects. There are many ways to go about dressing for a healthy bike ride.

It need not be in bright neon colors either. Outdoor recreationalists as a whole have moved away from the earth tone, 'let's blend in with nature' attitude, and have taken up the emblazoned, passionate colors. Bright purples and greens and oranges have in fact become the standard, and in a backcountry setting those colors can be intrusive to others.

When going for an extended trip, make sure you take extra clothes suitable for the conditions encountered. What those are is determined by the type and the length of the trip, the terrain to, and the season. Most people tend to take too much, and when biking, weight and available space is a concern. Find the right balance between being frugal and being prepared.

Chapter 8
_____ Backcountry Travel

Ah, the backcountry! There's no other place like it. Overall recreational use in our parks, national forests and on BLM (Bureau of Land Management) land keeps increasing. People in the United States spend 100 million days annually in national parks, and 235 million days annually in national forests. These figures are projected to increase geometrically as the twenty-first century approaches (*These American Lands*, Dyan Zaslowsky, 1986, p. 102).

This increase has led to heightened awareness of the environment — but not in proportion to the stress that larger numbers of people in the wilderness puts on the ecosystems. Recreationalists and non-recreationalists alike should be aware that although the outdoors may be a playground for many of us, it is the home and the very existence of innumerable fellow creatures. Indeed, it is the backbone of life on our planet.

With this in mind, here are some general guidelines to think about; these are conservation practices that help relieve human impact on the land and its inhabitants. It is especially important for mountain bikers. Mountain biking is still looked upon with suspicion by many environmentalists who see it as destructive towards the environment and obnoxious to other outdoor users. This viewpoint does have some basis in fact, and the more we can do to transform this opinion, the better off we and our sport will be.

When you must ride cross-country, do not ride single-file. Keep separate routes a good distance apart

Secondly, mountain biking can be very destructive if it is not executed with consideration of its impact on the environment: if you don't do it right, don't do it at all. Here's how to do it right:

☐ If you can choose your time, go into the backcountry when use levels are low, either off-season or during the week. Don't travel when the land can be rapidly degraded. To give an example, fat tires can do an incredible amount of damage when the trails are muddy from rain or snowmelt.

☐ Avoid using both high-impact areas that need a rest and undisturbed places that perhaps should remain left alone altogether. Have the respect and the awareness to be able to say, 'not here, not today.'

☐ Realize that wildlife not only needs to have undisturbed territory, but that the creatures themselves need to remain undisturbed. Never, under any circumstances, feed birds or other animals, even though they may be inquisitive or obviously used to handouts. Feeding wildlife can upset feeding habits, migration patterns, and reproduction levels. This can ultimately affect behavior, population structure, and species composition. If you stop to photograph or observe birds or other wildlife, stay downwind, avoid sudden movements, and respect their space by not harassing them. Stay away from birthing or nesting sites, feeding grounds and watering holes. Disturbance in these areas particularly stresses individual animals, and could affect their survival, especially during winter.

☐ Traveling quietly and in small groups (remember, four is the optimal number) will allow you to appreciate the environment more and will disturb wildlife and other visitors less. If you are with a large group, split up into smaller groups when you're biking, meeting back together later. Find the right balance between safety and minimum-impact travel.

☐ When traveling on existing trails, ride single-file on the designated path. Often there are several parallel trails. These are caused by hikers and bikers who move outside the original trail to avoid mud puddles, rocks, tree roots, or just in order to travel side-by-side for communication purposes. With a mountain bike you should be able to pop over those tree roots, splash through those puddles (after checking them out first). If Linda Goodman, the astrologer, is telling you 'not today,' then get off your bike and walk over or through those obstacles. Do your part to keep the trail from be-

Respect the environment: Don't ride on trails that will be negatively impacted by your use.

coming a four-lane expressway. If a trail is impassable, pick the best route around the problem area, trying to stay on hard surfaces such as rock, snowpack, or sand — and let the agency responsible for the area know that it should get their crew out there to maintain the trail. Don't shortcut trail switchbacks. This causes erosion and gullying.

☐ Cross-country travel is only acceptable when group size is small, when fragile areas can be avoided, and when wildlife will remain relatively undisturbed. Stay away from areas where undesignated trail systems are developing.

☐ When moving across land with no trail systems, it is usually better not to ride single file. By spreading out, you will avoid impacting vegetation. Extremely fragile areas, such as cryptogram soils in the desert, should really be avoided altogether, but if you do get out there, at least ride single file, so as to create only one narrow trail.

☐ In certain areas there is always the possibility of meeting lifestock on the trail. Horses and other stock are easily frightened; their comprehension is very limited when it comes to seeing the monster we call a bike with rider (or even hiker with backpack). In such cases, get off your bike slowly, get way off the trail, and give the animal plenty of room. Let the people with the animals be in charge of the situation. It is best to get on the downhill side of the trail, since when animals spook they usually jump uphill, and they are less frightened when you are below rather than above them. Sometimes it is recommended to talk in a low voice to give the animals advance notice of your whereabouts.

☐ When taking a break along the trail, move off to one side, far enough for the visual impact you create to be lessened. This way you and other parties can enjoy more solitude and more of the natural surroundings. Again, find areas to rest in that are not fragile — non-vegetated areas, such as rock outcroppings or snow patches, are preferred. On the other hand, some vegetation is actually very durable, so use your judgment.

☐ Pack out litter — your own as well as others', and dispose of it properly. This is easy enough to do on your way out, when your daypack or panniers are lighter.

☐ What is naturally found in the wilderness must be left there, whether it be organic or inorganic. Allow others the same chance of enjoying something unique and beautiful; let them have that same sense of discovery. At the same time, realize nature's intrinsic right to hold its own, without every visitor laying claim to one thing or another. This holds especially true for archaeological finds in the southwestern areas of the U.S., including arrow heads, pottery shards, and other remnants of history. Look at them, take pictures, feel their significance, and then leave them for professionals to use in putting together that area's past culture. You may want to mark the spot on your map and inform the appropriate agency, or you may want to leave it the way you found it, hoping it remains undisturbed.

Campsite Selection

The sun will set in a couple of hours, and you and your friends have just had an incredible day on the desert slickrock. It is time to start the tea brewing, the pasta water boiling, and to call some place home for the evening. Finding an aesthetic and proper place to bed down is a relatively simple and pleasant task, though finding a good minimum-impact site sometimes takes time. Making the right choice is an important ways to make sure your impact on the area is as little as possible. Expend the energy necessary to do it right. Here are a few considerations when looking for that perfect spot:

☐ Know the regulations. In regard to camping, there is a wide variance of protocol, even within the same land agency. Policies are dependent on land use priorities, location, and type of ecosystem. They are good guidelines to follow, and can help you when on private land as well.

☐ When selecting a campsite, distinguish between high-

Choose low-impact campsites. Don't camp within sight of the trail. Camp at least 200 feet away from high water tables, streams or lakes. Latrines should be at least 200 feet from your camp, as well as from the high water table. Do not disturb game trails: use different routes to and from the camp.

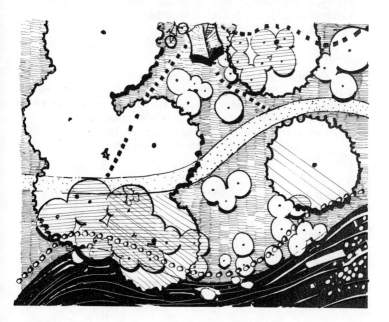

and low-impact sites, and choose accordingly.

In some high-use areas, it may be prudent to camp on an already highly-impacted area; with the right behavior, you and your party will do no further damage. When selecting a site like this, avoid enlarging the site by confining your tent and kitchen areas to already compacted areas. Stay on established traffic routes, and away from areas that are obviously undergoing rapid soil erosion.

Avoid lightly impacted sites. These are areas that have obviously been used but still maintain some vegetative integrity. If left alone, they will rejuvenate quickly. With continued use, however, they rapidly deteriorate beyond the point of recovery.

☐ Remember your relationship with the water. Streams and lakes can easily be contaminated by people moving, cooking and sleeping in close proximity to them. This can happen by dropping things into the water, or through runoff later on. People's close presence also inhibits wildlife from using their accustomed water sources. Camping a minimum of 200 feet away from water sources is required in many government-controlled areas, and it is a good practice to follow wherever you are.

☐ Don't camp on game trails. Sometimes they are obvious, other times obscure. Trails made by deer and other animals can be an acceptable route to follow while traveling (if they're going in your direction), but since many animals are nocturnal, camps should be a good distance away from such trails.

☐ For purely aesthetic reasons, camps should also be located away from designated biking or hiking trails, preferably out of sight altogether. Surely you would not be thrilled yourself when mountain biking in the wilderness to round a corner, exhilarated by the beauty of the scenery — only to be confronted with a tent right on the path.

☐ Think about the durability of the substrate you are on, and avoid the fragile ones. Grasses seem to be more tolerant than woody-stemmed plants and tree seedlings, but plants in general don't like to be camped on for very long. Forest duff (the layer of decomposing detritus which overlies the mineral soil) is a good choice, as is rock and snow.

☐ When looking for the perfect place for your tent, think flat (a slight concavity will collect rainwater), think high (for water runoff), and think safety. Be aware of potential hazards: standing dead trees, rockfall, flash flooding, wind and wind-carried debris. If you move rocks to stake down the tent, or move branches, pinecones, or other debris to accommodate comfort, put them back where they were found before you leave. Wipe out all traces of your presence.

☐ Spread your bikes and packs away from the tent, and away from each other's; this will prevent a lot of disturbance in a concentrated area, and will avoid creating a path which zeroes in on your sleeping quarters. Distributing your gear between your tent and your panniers, pack, or bike will also prevent you from having to run to the tent every time you need something.

☐ If you are going to stay in an area for an extended period of time, you may want to move your campsite every couple of days. Moving just a hundred yards away can make a lot of difference in terms of the environmental impact you have on an area.

☐ Keep your kitchen clean, and a fair distance (50-100 ft.) away from your bedding. This also minimizes your impact, and keeps night creatures away from you while you're in the snooze mode. Make sure your food is inaccessible to the local animal populations.

☐ All sites should be left as you found them — or better, if others have done damage before you. Don't dig trenches for tents, cut standing trees or their branches, pull up plants or embedded rocks. This is a quiet way of eco-defense, and is wise care.

Making Fires

Fires can be a fantastic source of enjoyment: What's a good story and a cup of coffee without some flames to gaze into once in a while? However, there is an appropriate place, time, and size for a fire — and a correct way for building it. Building a minimum-impact fire is fun and can be raised to an artistic level.

Before deciding on a fire, make sure that regulations allow it and that you are familiar with any restrictions. Double check the area, making sure it can supply an adequate source of fuel. There should be enough deadfall around that you can pick up what you need from the ground. If there is little deadfall available, or if you would need to take dead twigs from the surrounding trees, then you are not in an area suitable for fire building. The soil needs that deadfall, which is an important component of detritus build-up, leading to plant growth and wildlife habitation.

Areas that would not be appropriate are desert or alpine
environments, or even forested areas that have seen a lot
of use and/or abuse. Always be aware of fire hazard potential, keeping the fire away from tents, ground vegetation,
trees and their root and branch systems. Two methods of
fire building will be described below: the *mound fire* and
the *pit fire*. The mound fire is not your typical fire; it is an
ecologically sound alternative.

The Mound Fire

1. Once you have decided that it is OK to build a fire, find
    a good source of inorganic, or mineral, soil. River beds
    are excellent sources. Any soil that does not have a lot
    of dirt or organic material in it is satisfactory. You can
    transport this material by shovelling it into a stuff sack
    turned inside out.

2. Lay a thick layer of this soil out on a square of fire-
    proof material, which you can get at a good hardware
    store or outdoor shop. Usually this material comes in
    blanket sizes, which you can cut up. Layer this soil
    thick enough so that it, in combination with the
    fireproof material, insulates the ground underneath
    from getting scorched. The best places to put your fire
    would be on mineral soil, a flat rock, a thin layer of
    duff, or any other area where there is not much vegeta-
    tion.

3. Collect small twigs no longer than your hand and no
    thicker than your middle finger — and a good many
    that are even thinner.

4. When you are ready to dismantle the fire, burn all the
    wood down to white ash, which can be spread out
    around the ground or dispersed on a nearby river or
    creek once it has cooled. Return the inorganic soil to
    its proper place. This is much better than leaving the
    old campfire ring of blackened stones and half-charred
    wood.

The Pit Fire

This is another type of minimum impact fire, though in
many circles this method is not as favored as the mound
fire.

1. Dig a pit several inches deep in mineral soil, keeping
    the sides vertical and the pit shallow enough to allow
    for air circulation. Make sure there is no vegetation or
    duff surrounding the pit that could inadvertently catch
    on fire. You may want to place mineral soil around the
    perimeter and keep it moist.

2. When you start digging, remove any vegetation and its roots as gently and in as much of a single unit (soil, roots and plants) as possible, trying to keep the root system intact. Lay this aside several feet from the fire pit itself, keeping it moist with a cover of damp soil. Cover all of the roots.

3. Afterwards, clean up the same way you would a mound fire. Fill in the pit, and replace any vegetative block which you may have cut away. If there are any air pockets underneath or around the sod blocks, the soil will settle, leaving a depression, and/or roots will desiccate.

Because complete combustion is difficult, refrain from burning food scraps and non-wood material. This refuse is a pain to clean up, and heats the ground more than combustible wood.

Hygiene

This is where we get into what is for some still a delicate topic, namely that of human waste disposal. For others, more Freudian and less demure, the subject matter is one of insouciant delight. As more people frequent the outdoors, and stay out for longer periods of time, the more essential it is to understand and abide by guidelines for proper feces disposal. Here are some basic concepts as you strive for the most ecological way to lighten your load

1. Minimize the chance of an encounter between other people or animals and your feces ('It').

2. Minimize the chance that It will find its way to a water source.

3. Maximize the rate of its decomposition.

The first goal is most easily met by burying it in individual 'catholes,' though this does not guarantee that animals will not scent It and dig It up. Dig a small pit in a flat surface about six inches deep, making sure It is within an organic soil horizon. This ensures as much biological decomposition as possible. Breakdown will be minimal where the soil is cold, wet or sterile (inorganic). Be certain you are at least 200 feet away from the nearest water source, and that there is no surface moisture present where you are digging. Having kept the topsoil intact, replace it and camouflage the hole as necessary.

Unfortunately, buried feces do not decompose as quickly or thoroughly as most people believe. Regardless of burial depth or site location, pathogenic organisms within buried human waste can survive for as long as a year or more.

For this reason it is imperative that catholes are distributed well away from camp sites, trails, and any water
sources, both perennial and seasonal.

Solar radiation, wind and rain are the best agents that
promote decomposition. Although the majority of places
where we bike are not realistically remote enough to leave
deposits on the surface, this is the preferred method
where possible. In desert or alpine areas, organic soil is
ènot as abundant and elemental forces are strong, so this
method works well there. In an area where some fat tire or
sneaker is loathe to wander, scatter and smear It in a well-
exposed and dry area, where nature's forces can quickly
go to work.

As regards toilet paper, nature gives substitutes in abun-
dance. Once your sensibilities have been affronted by encountering soggy TP strung out under trees or left laying
around in supposedly inconspicuous places, it becomes
very easy to become dogmatic about the impropriety of its
use. Articles that can be used instead are bare sticks,
rocks in all shapes and sizes, and species specific
pinecones (provided you use them in the right direction).
Just pick your preferences, and after you're finished with
them, lightly chuck them in any wayward direction (as-
suming it is not toward water) — natural elements will
make quick work of them. The bigger the object you
choose, the greater chance you have of staying clean yourself. People who have never used these items in this way
before are usually quite surprised and pleased with the
way they perform. Snow is an excellent cleanser. Living
plant materials has some advantages and disadvantages.
But know your botany: there are lots of toxic plants out
there, and exposure in such a sensitive area can be out-
right dangerous or at least just plain uncomfortable. Although many leaf shapes can do a wonderful job for you,
think twice before uprooting a plant or defoliating it for
your personal sanitation.

If your constitution just doesn't allow for the natural way,
and you decide that TP is a must, bring along zip-lock baggies so that you can carry it out. It will not decompose
within a reasonable time frame if buried; it would be more
likely to be dug up by animals. And anyone who has tried
to burn used TP knows that it just doesn't work, and is
more of a hazard than it is worth. Tampons should also be
biked out with you, and never buried.

The only real concern with urination is that it attracts salt-
craved animals, who will dig up soil and plants to try and
consume what you have sprinkled around. Urinating on
rocks or inorganic soil prevents this problem.

One of the main concerns in all of this is to stay clean yourself. Soap is not naturally found outdoors, and its use is discouraged. The word *biodegradable* is a relative term, and has been cast about with abandon. Many things can be decomposed through biological processes given the right conditions, but it is often dubious that those conditions exist where presumably biodegradable products are used.

The best way to wash your hands — and you should wash them often when outside — is to use water and a lot of friction. Rubbing your hands together vigorously and rinsing well should do the job. If you do need to use a type of biodegradable soap, rinse them well away from lakes and streams so that it has time to break down and filter within the soil. The lower the temperature, the less biodegradation can take place.

Chapter 9
Orientation and
_____ Survival

When you get out into the backcountry, it will be imperative that you can find your way around. And if you do get
lost temporarily, you should know how to survive and get
back home safely. Using a map and compass is not an accomplished feat for many, yet not a particularly hard one
to master. The only sure way of becoming adept with these
two tools is to go outside and practice with them. Your ex-
periences will give you more than a book or article can attempt to teach you. In this section, I want to whet your appetite and hopefully motivate you to seek resources that
are exclusively dedicated to map and compass use.

Maps
There are several types of maps you are likely to encounter
while planning for a mountain bike trip onto public land.
The most common, the most reliable, and probably the
most suitable is the topographic map, from *topo* meaning
'place' in Greek, and *graphein* 'write' or 'draw.' When talking about topographic maps, I will be referring to the
USGS (U.S. Geological Survey) maps, which are considered reliable and quite accessible.

Topographical map are give a three-dimensional repre-
sentation of the land's physical features in a two-dimen-
sional format. This is done with the aid of contour lines,
with each line designating points of equal elevation. Every
fifth contour line is colored a heavier brown than the
others, and is the index contour, with the exact elevation
written somewhere along the line. The contour interval between the lines shows elevation gain or loss and the steep-
ness of the grade, depending on how close together the
contour lines are. A flat meadow would have contour lines
relatively far apart, while a steep slope would be illustrated with the lines tightly packed together. The contour
interval is designated at the bottom of the map (i.e. 20 or
40 feet). To find the slope percentage between contours, to
divide the contour interval (vertical distance in feet between contours) by their horizontal distance apart and
multiply by one hundred. What this number tells you is
the how many vertical feet you travel for every 100 feet
traveled horizontally.

Topographic map are sometimes called a quadrangles, or
quads: due to the curvature of the earth they are not true

rectangles. As part of the Geographic Grid system, each topo shows its specific location on the earth. The top of the map is always north, the bottom south, making the right east and the left west.

Latitude and longitude numbers are given in each corner of the map. Parallels, or lines of latitude, run east to west geographically. They intersect lines of longitude, or meridians, which run geographically north to south, at right angles. The First Meridian, 0 degree longitude, is located at Greenwich, England and all other meridians run in degrees, minutes, and seconds east and west of this location. One hundred and eighty degrees away in either direction from Greenwich is the International Date Line, exactly half way around the world.

Parallels begin at the Equator, which is 0 degree latitude. North and south of this line, parallels run in degrees, minutes, and seconds towards the earth's poles, which are both located at 90 degrees. Crested Butte, Colorado, one of the mountain biking capitals of the world, is located at longitude 106.59 W, latitude 38.52 N. One degree corresponds to 60 minutes, one minute to 60 seconds. Because topo maps are categorized according to the fraction of the earth's curvature they cover, they will be designated accordingly. Most topographic maps are on half of a degree (30 minutes), one quarter of a degree (15 minutes), or one eighth of a degree (7.5 minutes). The designation for this is in the upper right corner under the name of the map. You can verify this number by comparing the difference between the longitude or latitude numbers in the corners.

There will be a scale explaining what one unit on the map is in relation to one unit on the actual landscape. This scale can be found in the lower center of the map, and its ratio depends on what degree of map you're using. For instance, the scale for a 15 minute series map is 1:62,500: for every one unit of distance on the map, there are 62,500 units to cover the distance on the earth. One inch on this quad represents approximately 5208.3 feet (slightly less than a mile) in the field.

The the smaller the the denominator (the second figure) of the scale, the larger the relief features on the map will appear, and the more detail is available. The denominator 24,000 (the scale for a 7.5 minute map) is smaller than that of a 1:62,500 map, and so will yield more detail. The more detailed the map, the less land can be covered on that one sheet. A good map for off-road biking might be a 7.5 minute map.

There is a quadrangle location map showing where this particular quad is in relation to the state in the lower right-hand corner of each topo map. The names of adjoining quads are shown along each edge and in the corners of the quad proper.

Different colors and symbols are used on topographic maps to represent land features and objects, respectively. Blue represents hydrographic features like lakes, streams, rivers, swamps, snow and ice. Brown designates the hypsographic features, represented by contour lines and contour indexes. Green represents vegetated areas dense enough to hide a platoon (27 people) from aerial observation in one acre. Conversely, white indicates areas of little or no vegetation, and includes boulder fields, meadows, and non-timbered areas above treeline. Black indicates anything named, made, or designated by homo sapiens. Buildings, borders of public and civic lands, benchmarks, the names of ridges, lakes, mountains all these are black. Red is part of the U.S. Public Land Survey Grid, more commonly known as the township and range system, used mainly for surveying purposes. 'Important' roads are also shown in red.

Purple is used to show revisions made since the last dated issue of the map, making it a very important color, and one that a lot of people don't pay as much attention to as they should. A quad's date of issue (in black) can be found on the right side of the bottom margin of the map, printed beneath the quadrangle name. In most cases that date is 'dated,' the map having been surveyed from the air and issued quite a while ago. In the years that followed, many pertinent changes may have take place, and those have been recorded in purple. This means that field checks of aerial updates have not yet been done. Many times changes have occured which have not even found their way into purple ink yet, so look at that issue date and realize that it may not be as accurate as it once was, particularly as regards man-made features. Trails, roads, junctions, land ownership, all these things may not be the way they once were.

Learning to use a topographic map takes concentrated time, and lots of it. To the well-trained eye, these maps reveal an astonishing amount of information. The best advice is to take a topo map of a favorite and close-by biking haunt of yours, go to it, read the landscape and superimpose it on the map. Find the relationship between the two. Learn to recognize what a ridgeline, or a valley looks like on paper. Do contour lines in drainages point up, towards higher elevation, or down? Look at a steep hill: what does

it look like on the map? Feel the spatial relationship between a particular scale of map and the actual terrain.

With the knowledge and experience you gain from intimacy with the map, will help you find your way. Time
Control Plans will also help you in this effort. Here are
some additional points that will help you in the route-finding process.

☐ Orient you map: So often people use their map trying to
   place terrain features with what they're seeing on the
   map, they're looking North while their map is facing
   West! Find True North, and then lay your map out so
   that North on the map is actually facing the day's
   North. Now the direction of features you are sur-
   rounded by corresponds with that of the same features
   on the map.

☐ Use what is known in the orienteering world as 'collecting features' as points of reference while traveling. This
   can be especially important when mountain biking
   since being on two wheels allows you to move rather
   rapidly, and if you are not paying attention, you may
   lose your way only too easily. Collecting features are
   simply those landmarks that pave the way to a specific
   destination. Streams, benchmarks, ridgelines, open
   meadows, can all be collecting features. Make notes of
   them, mental or otherwise, and be aware as you pass
   them by on the way to your final destination: use them
   as points of reference. Don't let tunnel vision of that
   cabin you're heading to obscure the journey. Instead,
   tick off the collecting features as you travel along —
   'Okay, we've come to that intermittent stream we
   noticed on the map. That means we head north along it
   until....' 'If we hit this ridgeline we've gone too far....'

☐ Use 'handrails,' which are any linear features, natural
   or artificial, to follow until they no longer point the
   direction you're going. Streams, fences, roads, trails,
   and valley-bottoms are good handrails.

☐ As you're riding, look back every once in a while in the
   direction you're coming from. Pick out salient
   landmarks. Landscape features can look very different
   from the opposite direction. If you need to backtrack for
   any reason, this technique will assist you in confirming
   that you're on the right track.

☐ Keep your map readily available so that you will use it:
   It is like the water bottle, which you are most likely to
   use if it is within easy reach. Keep the map in zip-lock
   bag to protect it and fold it to show the area you're in.

Besides the topo, there is another type of map you may run into and find useful. The U.S. Forest Service puts out its own maps of the national forests. They may well be more up to date than USGS maps, especially in terms of trail systems. However, they are usually based on USGS originals, and as such can be full of reproductive inaccuracies like misalignment or freehand additions.

Both the Forest Service and the Bureau of Land Management (BLM) put out recreational maps which cover an entire forest or BLM holding. These are not in topographic format, and they are limited in their usefulness for detailed route-finding because they are on such a large scale. They do give a nice overview of the area, though, and are handy to have as an all-purpose map for trip planning.

Obtaining Maps

Local area outdoor stores will more than likely carry the state's USGS topographic maps. If they don't, or if you need topos of another state or maps of BLM holdings, you may ask for assistance and order maps from the Denver office: ·

U.S. Geological Survey
Federal Center
P.O. Box 25286
Denver CO 80225
Tel.: (303) 236-7477

They will send you a state index grid identifying a state's topo maps by name and location free of charge. Any special topos that are available (those for a national monument, for instance) will also be included in the index. You might also ask for a pamphlet called *Topographic Map Symbols*, which lists and explains all the symbols used on USGS maps, but which aren't necessarily all included on the legends of individual maps.

Once you know what you want, order from the above address and number. Order by mail. Individual quads cost $2.50 each, one of the last great bargains left in this day and age. Until recently there was an eastern and western distribution branch for the USGS, and you ordered from one branch or the other according to whether the maps you wanted were East or West of the Mississippi River. That has changed. For *all* areas, East and West of the Mississippi River, including Alaska, Hawaii, America Samoa, Guam, Puerto Rico, the Virgin Islands of the United States, and Antarctica, collect information and maps from Denver. Alaskan residents can also order an index and maps of the 49th state from:

Alaska Distribution Section U.S. Geological Survey
New Federal Building
P.O. Box 12
101 Twelfth Avenue, Fairbanks AK 99701
Tel.: (907)456-0244.

Two more sources of topo maps, with prepayment necessary, are:

Timely Discount Topos
Jeffco Airport Executive Building
9769 West 119th Drive # 9
Broomfield CO 80020
Tel.: (800) 821-7609

Defense Mapping Agency
Office of Distribution Services
Washington DC 20215-0010
Tel.: (202) 227-2445, or (202) 653-1478

To obtain maps for a national forest area, contact:
U.S. Forest Service Information Office
Room 3238
PO Box 2417
Washington DC 20013
Tel.: (202) 447-3760

The Compass

Almost everyone has a compass stashed away in a drawer
somewhere, but the percentage of people who know how to
use them well is small. These instruments have been
around since Chinese and Mediterranean navigators
floated simple pieces of magnetic iron on straw or cork in
a bowl of water, around 1100 AD. Since then the instruments have come a long way in the area of precision. The
know-how to use them has become a very competitive
sport known as orienteering.

Knowing how to use a compass is a good skill to have. Although you will not often need to use one, it is nice to
have the skill when the need arises. As a substitute you
can use the angle of the sun. Being able to figure out the
direction from the angle of the sun is not as difficult as it
would at first seem. Paying attention to the sun consistent-
ly, so you become acquainted with it, is the hardest part.
We tend to enclose ourselves in four walls and a ceiling so
often that we do not make a habit of gazing towards the
sky. Once you do start to do so, however, you'll find that
the sun is very consistent and faithful: it really does 'rise'
in the east and 'set' in the west, keeping a southern orien-

tation here in the northern hemisphere. When you're out riding, practice figuring out the direction and guessing the time of day by just looking at the sun. Verify your estimate with the aid of the compass and your watch. It doesn't take long to become fairly accurate.

An orienteering compass consists of three basic parts:

1. Magnetic tipped needle — the red end always points toward the magnetic North Pole.

2. Compass housing marked with an orienteering arrow and orienting lines, with a graduated 360 degree dial marked around the compass housing. The bearing is read at the index pointer.

3. A baseplate marked with the direction-of-travel arrow, and the index pointer.

There are two basic ways of using a magnetic compass: from map to terrain, or from terrain to map. It will help you to visualize the map bearing process if you take out a map and compass while you learn.

In going from map to terrain, you are usually taking map bearings, or true bearings. To indicate direction in the field, two basic conditions must be met:

1. Set the dial to the desired degree reading. If the degree or direction is known, simply turn the dial so that the correct reading appears at the index pointer.

2. Without changing the dial setting, position the entire compass so that the orienting arrow is in line with the magnetic needle and the red end of the needle lies between the two orienting points. Your line of travel will follow the sighting line on your compass. As long as you keep the magnetic needle 'boxed' within the orienting arrow, you're set to travel in the direction of your sighting line. Some higher quality compasses have a mirror with a sighting line for extreme accuracy, with accompanying directions on how to use it.

To obtain your bearing from a map, lay your compass on the map with the baseplate parallel to the line on the map upon which you wish to travel. Next, hold the compass in position on the map, and turn the dial so the meridian lines on the compass are exactly parallel with any meridian line on the map, and the letter N on top of the dial is toward North on the map. This has now set the degree reading to your destination. Read at the index pointer. Now use the compass by the sighting line or by sight.

If you want to take a bearing from the terrain, simply hold

the compass in front of you, with the sighting line pointing in front of you. Pivot yourself and the compass around together as one unit until the sighting line points toward the object on which you are taking the bearing. Turn the graduating dial until the orienting arrow and the magnetic needle are lined up, or 'boxed,' with the red end of the needle lying between the two orienting points. The degree reading at the index pointer is the bearing you want to take.

Declination

You can't mention map and compass without talking at least a little bit about *declination*. It is generally known that Magnetic North is not the same as the True North Pole. For now, Magnetic North is located near Bathurst Island in northern Canada, and continually moves around (in geologic terms) as the earth's magnetic lines of force change position.

Maps and directions are almost always based on True North, which is static. Magnetic declination is the angle between these two points. Where True North and Magnetic North are in the same direction, the declination is therefore zero. The line of zero declination in North America runs West of Hudson Bay down along Lake Michigan to the Gulf Coast in western Florida. At any point West of that line, a compass needle will point East of True North, or in an *Easterly Declination*. *Westerly Declination* is any point which is East of the zero declination line. In North America, magnetic declination varies from 30 degrees east in Alaska to 30 degrees west in Labrador.

On topographic maps, declination is given in the bottom left corner. If you want to use a compass with your map, and need to take declination into account, there are two ways you can do so. The easiest way is to draw lines of magnetic declination on the map before entering the field. Just take a straightedge and extend the degree of declination line up through the center of the map. With this line as your guide, continue drawing Magnetic North lines one inch apart across the entire surface of the map. You now no longer need to compensate for declination because these lines correspond precisely to the compass needle.

If you would rather adjust your map bearings for declination mathematically, it is very simple. First, look on the map to find what the declination is in your area. Then, take your bearing as you normally would; your degree reading will be at the index pointer. If the declination of your area is Easterly, decrease the dial reading by the amount of declination. If Westerly, increase the reading.

If you learn the few skills mentioned here you will be able to use a compass in many different situations. If you want to continue your education in both map and compass, one of the best books on the market is Bjorn Kjellstrom's, *Be Expert With Map and Compass, The Orienteering Handbook* (Charles Scribner Sons). It begins at an elementary level and proceeds to the most skilled levels of orienteering. Excellent exercises and tools are included.

For more information on orienteering teaching aids and equipment, you can contact:
Orienteering Services USA
PO Box 1604
Binghamton NY 13902
Tel.: (607) 724-0411.

There are three major companies that make solid, reliable compasses, in a wide spectrum of models and prices. They are:

The Brunton Company
620 East Monroe
Riverton WY 82501
Tel.: (307) 865-6559

Silva Johnson Camping Inc.
PO Box 966
Binghamton NY 13902
Tel.: (607) 779-2200

Suunto USA
2151 Las Palmas Drive
Carlsbad CA 92009
Tel.: (619) 931-6788

When You Get Lost

As one outdoorsman noted, "While the process of becoming lost is usually a lot of fun, the entertainment value diminishes rapidly once the act is accomplished" (Patrick F. McManus, *A Fine and Pleasant Misery*, p. 16). There can be a number of dimensions involved in getting lost, but action to be taken once it is a *fait accompli* is somewhat limited. The key, obviously, is not to to get lost in the first place. This is best accomplished with careful map work in conjunction with thoughtful movement. This can be hard to do on a bike because so much ground can be covered so rapidly. Follow your progress on the map, orienting it whenever you change direction and referencing the major land features in the terrain with their locations on the map.

Some people like to build *cairns*, piles of rocks that mark their way. If unusual circumstances require that you mark your passage, cairns can be a good way to go. It is important, however, that once you've established where you are, or are on your return trip, that you dismantle any cairn you build. There is no need for them to remain standing, and they take away other people's sense of adventure and solitude. The use of a TCP, as described in Chapter 7, should make construction of carins unnecessary in most cases. Any permanent type of marking, such as blazing a tree, should to be avoided. Only an emergency situation would warrant such an action.

If you are irrevocably lost, the first thing to do is to acknowledge the fact and save yourself a lot of *angst* and energy. Once a state of 'lostness' has been acknowledged, you can move on to much more pressing and important needs, such as taking care of yourself and those with you.

There is a difference between being prepared and knowing how to survive. Being prepared means relying on your common sense, past experience and equipment to take you through any unexpected twists you may encounter. It is important to be comfortable and safe, and enjoy the outdoors without impacting it. Being lost doesn't change any of those basic premises that you start out with. Barring exceptional circumstances, you still have your layers of clothing, your wits and common sense, the first-aid kit and the skills to perform first aid, water, food, and either artificial shelter or whatever nature can provide. Somebody has your TCP and knows your whereabouts. All you need to do is to continue to take good care of yourself and keep panic at bay. A sense of humor is one of the best ways to do so. Next, wait for help.

If you feel fairly confident that you can retrace your movements and find your way again, you might opt to do so, being careful not to get so far away from your original position that you figure 'they'll never think of looking for me over here.' Even when you're lost, you are a better target when stationary than when you are continually and erratically careening about. In this case, being lost isn't such a horrible thing. Do not expect it, but anticipate that it could happen, and be prepared for it.

Knowing how to survive is a completely different matter. Survival entails knowing how to live off what's left of the fat of the land. In this scenario, you take and use whatever you can from nature to ensure your continuance. It is not a minimum impact method, nor is it technologically oriented. It makes sense to take specific training in survival skills. Once you are lost, you are usually not in the best of mindsets to test your amateur survival instincts, or to try out the survival methods outlined in a book. There are some excellent outdoor survival schools throughout the country, and I suggest you look into them well in advance if you expect to need survival skills.

Food Rationing

When going on an extended bike tout, whether on the road or in the backcountry, there are some considerations in regards to munchies. Because of the unique style of travel, two of the main limiting factors bicyclists face are weight and available space. Here are some points to consider when planning what delectables will accompany, nourish, and satisfy you along the way.

Energy content:
Choose foods that are high in carbohydrates.

Nutritional balance:
Strive for some balance between the four food groups and their substitutes.

Purpose of trip:
The goals of your bike ride should dictate to some extent the type of food you take along. Are you out for some fast touring, where you want to make tracks and see some country? Then your food should be simple and easy to prepare. If it is more of a relaxed trip and meal preparation time is not as important, you might want to have foods that will make more sophisticated meals.

Weight:
This is a priority concern. Many people feel dehydrated food is the way to go. It is extremely light, doesn't take up a lot of space, and is very easy to prepare. Add a little water and poof, some semblance of steak Diane is on the plate. The disadvantage of freeze-dried food is that it can be prohibitively expensive and often tastes terrible. There are many regular dried foods in your local grocery store that are light weight, easy to cook, and with considerable more taste.

Spoilage:
Think about not only the length of your trip but also the general climatic and seasonal conditions you'll encounter.

Expense and availability:
There are many things you can do to cut down the cost. Don't buy freeze-dried foods. Cooking from scratch, and eliminating 'box' dinners and casseroles is also less expensive. Supplement meats with cereal, legumes, cheese, and dried milk combinations. Soybean products are reasonably priced and come in many palatable varieties. Don't

forget to compare prices.

Ease of packaging and handling:
Many goodies come in glass or metal containers, or are individually wrapped. Discard these wasteful packages, and consolidate your food in baggies or plastic containers. Reusable containers are light, convenient and they cut down on the amount of trash you end up biking out.

Variety:
Have you ever gone out on a trip with someone who wants to eat oatmeal every morning for breakfast? 'Simple, and good for you,' is his or her rationale. But not good for your morale: Depending on your strength of character, it can sometimes take only a very short time before depression and ambivalent feelings about your comrade sets in. Variety can be a key element in keeping energy in your body and that harmony between you and your companions.

Preparation:
There are simply prepared one-pot meals, as well as dishes that take a little more effort, equipment, and weight. Plan ahead for the style you prefer.

Available wild foods:
The joys of being in the backcountry is enhanced if you have knowledge of the ecosystem and its component parts. Being able to identify edible plants can be a real source of pleasure. It is fun to put huckleberries in the morning's pancakes. Be careful not to deplete an entire plant community in your zest for wild strawberries, though. Know what species might be rare, and use discretion to pass them by.

Quantities:
The amount of food to take on a trip varies with the type of trip and the kind of eater you are. Some people never get their fill, others are more moderate in their appetite. People who exercise moderately in the outdoors for extended periods of time usually eat approximately 1½ to 2 pounds per person per day, or 2500—3000 calories. If you bike strenuously, you may consume as much as 3000—3700 calories a day, or 2 to 2½ pounds per day.

Rations should also be readjusted for high altitude mountain bike trips in such areas like the Colorado or Canadian Rockies. The higher the altitude, the less oxygen is available for the metabolization of food. Since protein and fat become harder to digest, take just enough food rich in these nutrients to meet your needs. Also, the colder the environment, the more soup bases or drink mixes you might want to take, since these hot drinks provide both the extra warmth and water you will need.

Camp Stoves and Fuel

Most people now use efficient lightweight stoves for out-door cooking. Fuel use should be regulated wisely: the amount to be brought along should be estimated accurately so that fuel is not wasted and extra weight is not toted around unnecessarily — without running out before the end of the trip. Approximately one pint per stove per day will be sufficient fuel. If you and a couple of friends take an eight day trip, and use two stoves, you will need around eight quarts of fuel, or two gallons (2 stoves x 8 days = 16 pints, or 8 quarts). If you're planning a longer trip with more people, one quart for six person-days is a good equation to use in figuring out how much fuel is needed. So for a two-week road tour with 10 people (10 people x 14 days = 140 person-days), you'll need 140 / 6 = 23.3 quarts, or approximately six gallons.

Allow for more fuel consumption on cold days, when the quantity of warm food and drink needed increases. When going on this long of a road trip, it makes sense to buy things along the way wherever available, or to leave caches or boxes of supplies at points along the route. Marking boxes *General Delivery* and mailing them to post offices in the towns you will be going through works well; let the post master know how long the boxes should be kept, after which time they can send them back to the return address. Distribute your goods between all boxes sent, so if one is lost, you have not lost all your fuel, or all your peanut M&M's.

Chapter 10
Mountain Bike
Maintenance

With proper maintenance, a mountain bike will last many years, perhaps a lifetime. The bicycle industry advertisers, just as the auto industry, have everyone believing that their products are obsolete, and should be replaced yearly, to be sure you have what is newest and best. What they don't tell you is that current bicycle technology, while advancing, has actually been with us for a number of years. Most parts and materials used today are very similar to those used 40 years ago and will still work many years from now.

The most obvious reason to maintain your mountain bike is to keep it safe and enjoyable to ride. Nothing is more annoying and unsafe than a component that does not work properly when you are out in the middle of nowhere, trying to have a good time.

The information provided in this chapter covers many of the currently available as well as earlier parts. In the rapidly changing world of mountain bike components, not every operation can be discussed in detail, but the most general ones are.

Tightening and Loosening Mechanisms

Mechanical components are held together with nuts and bolts or other threaded parts. If overtightened or improperly assembled, threads can be irreparably damaged. The number one cause of thread damage is overtightening. It is always better to assemble a part, go for a short ride, recheck and only then tighten down anything loose, than to overtighten, stripping the threads and having more problems. When assembling two threaded parts, tighten them only to where one part fits snugly into the other. The most comprehensive bicycle maintenance manuals actually specify the torque to which certain bolts should to be tightened, but you can avoid most problems by developing a feel for how tight is tight enough for a certain size nut or bolt.

Misalignment of the threads during assembly can cause thread damage. Be patient when assembling two parts. Start by cleaning the parts and lightly spray them with silicon-based lubricant. This will keep water out and assist in subsequent as-

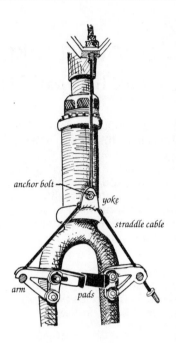

Cantilever brake

hand, stop. You've either misaligned the threads, or the threads are dirty, damaged, or improperly machined to begin with. To help align the threads properly, turn the part gently counterclockwise before turning it clockwise to tighten it.

If a part is difficult to remove, stop and think for a minute before you proceed. The parts could either be corroded, previously overtightened or reverse threaded. Corroded parts can be a real problem. The best way to free such a connection is to soak the parts with derusting fluid for at least 24 hours. Use a minimum amount of derusting fluid, just a couple of drops.

sembly or disassembly. Inspect the threads for wear and flat spots before assembly. A die can sometimes help straighten and clear the threads on a marginal part (ask at the bike shop), but seriously damaged parts should be replaced.

When you're ready to assemble the parts, concentrate on getting the threads aligned correctly. Begin tightening by hand, rather than with a tool, to make sure you don't force things. Most parts can be tightened quite a bit by hand before a tool is needed. If you can't tighten it very much using your

Brakes

Since mountain bikes are often ridden over very rugged terrain, they need more stopping power than road bikes. The brakes on a

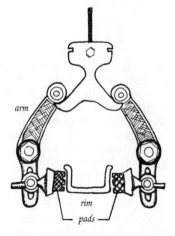

Roller-cam brake

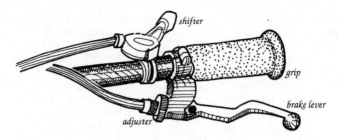

Shifter and brake lever

mountain bike consist of two brake arms, each with a brake pad, per wheel. When the brake lever is squeezed , the pads press against the sides of the wheel rim, resisting forward movement. The pads and brake cables are the two points of maintenance in the braking system.

Brake Pads

The brake pads must be replaced whenever they are worn to the point where the grooves in the pad are no longer recessed. These grooves allow water and debris to run off the pad surface.

To replace the pads, first release the straddle cable by squeezing the pads together and twisting the nipple out of one of the brake arms. Then loosen the nuts holding the brake pads on the brake arms. Remove the old pads and install the new pads, hand-tightening the nuts. Brake pads with arrows should be installed so the arrow points in the direction of wheel rotation.

Pads should be nearly parallel to the wheel rim, but the front of the pad should contact the rim one to two millimeters (about the thickness of a quarter) before the rear of the pad. This will prevent the brake from squealing like a pig when it is applied. Manipulate the pad until it is aligned, then hold it and tighten the nut. (This is a trial-and-error process: often the adjustment changes as you tighten the nut.) Squeeze the pads together and reconnect the straddle cable.

As the new pads are thicker than the old, worn ones, it may be necessary to loosen the anchor bolt and slacken the cable in order to reconnect the straddle cable.

Cables

A cable must be replaced if it is frayed. To do this, release the straddle cable, then loosen the cable anchor bolt. Pull the cable through the housing and free the nipple at the brake lever.

Apply a small amount of grease to the new cable before installing it, to ensure smooth operation. Insert the cable end with the nipple in the lever, push the rest of the cable through the housing and through the hole in the anchor bolt. Before tightening the anchor bolt, take the slack out of the cable. Ask a friend to squeeze the brake pads together while you pull the cable taut and tighten the anchor bolt. If you are alone, a tool called a 'third hand' can be used to hold the brake pads together. Squeeze the brake lever and test the cable adjustment. If the brake can't be forced hard down on the rim, the cable must be adjusted tighter. Lift the bike

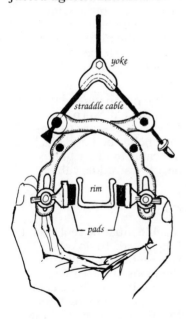

Releasing straddle cable on U-Brake

and spin the wheel to make sure the pads don't rub on the rim. Prior to riding, check your brakes by riding in a safe place, applying a little pressure at first, and then slowly more pressure in a series of stops to test the soundness of the brakes. If you are able to leave two black marks behind your tires when you have stopped, you have a brake system that works.

Wheels

Each wheel consists of a hub, spokes, a rim, a tire and an inner tube. Each of these components must be inspected separately to ensure a safe ride. To do this, remove the wheels from the bicycle, either by loosening the axle nuts, or by undoing the quick-release skewer outward. Some bicycles have ridges on the fork dropouts to prevent the front wheel from accidentally falling off. If your bicycle is so equipped, turn the skewer nut counter-clockwise until the wheel comes out. Remember to tighten the nut when reinstalling the wheel. (It may be necessary to release the brakes by unhooking the straddle cable in order to remove the wheel. See the *Brakes* section for this procedure.)

Hubs

Check the hub adjustment by trying to move the axle back and forth. If you feel play, the hub bearings are too loose. If there is no play, turn the axle several times with your fingers. It should spin freely and easily. If you feel excessive roughness, the bearings are too tight.

To adjust the hub bearings, first tighten the locknut and cone against each other on one side of the hub. Then adjust the hub from the other side by first backing the locknut away from the cone, and then turning the cone clockwise to tighten the bearing, or counter-clockwise to loosen it. Hold the cone in place on the axle and tighten the locknut against the cone. Repeat this procedure until the axle spins freely without excessive roughness. If, after numerous attempts, it turns out the hub just can't be adjusted correctly, it may have to be overhauled, which the bike shop can do for you.

Spokes and Freewheel

Inspect the spokes by squeezing them together in pairs. A broken one will be obvious and should be re-placed, while noticeably loose spokes should be tightened.

To replace a spoke, remove the tire and the tube. If the broken spoke is on the RH side of the rear wheel, the freewheel will have to be removed before the spoke can be replaced. This re-quires a freewheel remover tool, and a vice or a very large adjustable wrench. In-sert the freewheel tool into the freewheel and turn it counterclockwise until the freewheel comes away from the hub.

Some bikes have casette hubs, which incorporate a freewheel mechanism rather than a separate one. To remove the cogs on a casaette hub, put one sprocket removal tool ('whip') on the smallest cog, the other on the third or fourth cog. Use the first whip to turn the smallest cog counterclockwise. Once it has been removed, the other cogs pull straight off.

Hyperglide cogs requre one whip and a freewheel tool. Insert the freewheel tool in

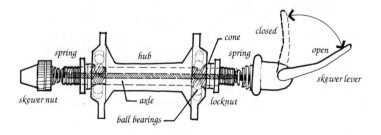

Quick-release hub

the lockring and use the whip to hold the other cogs while you turn the freewheel tool counterclockwise. The cogs will come straight off.

A bicycle shop can remove your freewheel for a small fee if you do not have the right tools. Remove the broken spoke and nipple and replace both. Apply some grease to the threads of the freewheel and thread it onto the hub by hand. It will tighten itself later as you pedal. Now the rim probably has to be trued, as described in the next section.

Rims

Check the rim to see if it is straight, or true, by spinning the wheel. If there are any major bends or curves in the rim then it must be trued. To do this, put the wheel back on the bicycle. Use the brake pads as a reference to find the exact place where the rim is bent (one of the pads will rub, or at least come much closer to the side of the rim, in the bent area). Use a spoke wrench to tighten the nipples on the inside of the bend and loosen them on the outside. Turn the spoke wrench approximately 1/4 turn at a time. Spin the wheel to check for improvement. Continue this process until the rim is true.

Tires and Tubes

Tires should be closely inspected at least weekly. If you see any cuts or fraying on the sidewalls, or any conspicuous bulges anywhere else, the tire should be replaced. If the tire is flat, and does not hold the air when inflated, the tube must be repaired or replaced. Deflate it completely, then use tire levers to pry one side of the tire over the edge of the rim. Pull the tube out from under the tire and pull the rest of the tire off the rim. Replace or repair the tire or tube as necessary.

If the tube was flat, you must carefully feel inside the tire until you find whatever caused the flat and remove it. Unless the object has severely cut the tire, the tire does not need to be replaced. Before reinstalling the tire and the tube, be sure that the rubber or plastic tape that covers the spoke nipples is in place. This tape protects the underside of the tube from any sharp edges on the rim and the nipples. Inflate the replacement (or patched) tube just enough to give it shape. Place the tube inside the tire, put the valve through the hole in the rim and put one side of the tire over the edge of the rim. Push the tube in place under the tire on the rim, and let the air escape through the valve. Then push the other side of the tire onto the rim. This will become difficult at the end, and you will be tempted to use a tire lever to pry the last bit over the edge: *don't do it!* That would puncture the tube and you would have to do the entire job over again. Instead, try to force more air out of the tube and keep trying.

Bottom Bracket

Check the crankarm bolts and pedals for tightness about once a week. Use a crank bolt tool or a 14 or 15 millimeter socket wrench to turn the bolts clockwise. Use a 15 millimeter open-end wrench for the pedals. The right pedal has a standard thread, but the left pedal has left-hand thread, so it must be turned counterclockwise to tighten it. Inspect each chainring for any broken or bent teeth by sighting along each chain ring as you slowly turn the cranks backwards.

The bottom bracket is the bearing assembly to which the crank arms are attached. The adjustment of these bearings should also be checked frequently. To do this, first pull the chain off the front chainring. Then grasp one crank arm in each hand near the pedal and rock them from side to side. If you feel play, the bottom bracket bearings are too loose. If there is no lateral movement at all, spin the crank arms and watch as they come to rest. They should slow and stop evenly with minimal surges

or jerks. If they don't, the bottom bracket bearings are too tight.

The bottom bracket is always adjusted from the LH side of the bike. To do this, loosen the lockring with a lockring tool. Then use a bottom bracket spanner to turn the adjustable cup clockwise to tighten the bottom bracket bearings and reduce play, or counterclockwise to loosen them. Only turn the adjustable cup $\frac{1}{16}$ to $\frac{1}{8}$ of a turn. Now hold the adjustable cup in place with the spanner and tighten the lockring. Check the adjustment as described above and repeat as necessary. If you just can't seem to get a good adjustment, there may be dirt or water inside the bottom bracket. In this case, take your bicycle to the bike shop to have the bottom bracket overhauled. Do not ride more than a day with a tight or loose bottom bracket.

Chain

A clean, well lubricated chain is essential for the smooth operation of the bicycle. If your chain appears dry, lightly coat it with chain lubricant. If you can't see the individual links at all, the chain has to be cleaned. To do this, first shift into the gear with the chain on the smallest cog and the smallest chainring. To remove the chain, put a link of the chain on the first position of the chain tool,

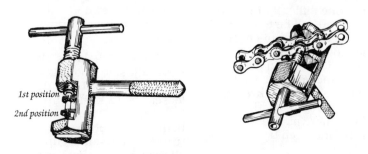

Left, chain tool. Right, The pin in the chain tool pushes the chain rivet
through the links

and turn the handle until the tool's pin touches the link's rivet. Now count six clockwise turns of the handle, making certain the pin and rivet are lined up. Back the tool away from the link and bend the chain laterally until it comes apart.

Pull the chain through the derailleurs and clean it in a solvent (gasoline or kerosene is not recommended — there are now biodegradable solvents for your bike). Wipe the chain dry and feed it through the derailleurs and around the

smallest cog and chainring. Put the link back together, and then use the first position of the chain tool to push the rivet back into place, again counting six turns. Feel both sides of the link simultaneously to ensure that the rivet is centered in the link. Lightly lubricate the entire chain, and test it for any stiff links.

To test for stiff links, turn the cranks slowly backwards. The chain should pass over the cogs and through the rear derailleur without skipping or jump-

As you turn the handle, make sure you do not push the pin all the way out

Then use the tool to push the pin back when the ends of the chain are joined

one link

The pin must stay in the outermost link unless your chain is of the Hyperglide type (see text)

ing over any teeth. If it
does, find the uncoopera-
tive link and put it in the
second position of your
chain tool. Turn the handle
about ⅙ of a turn to apply
a small amount of force on
the rivet. Repeat this until
all stiff links are relaxed. If
a stiff link refuses to relax
or a link appears
dangerously loose, it should
be replaced. Use the chain
removing procedure to do
this. Spare links can be pur-
chased at bike shops — but
make sure you get links
that match your particular
chain. If your bike has a Hyperglide chain, the rivet

must be pushed out com-
pletely and replaced by a
new one. Replacement
rivets are also available at
bike shops.

Derailleurs

To check the rear derail-
leur, shift the chain to the
smallest chainring and the
largest cog. Stand behind
the bicycle and make sure
the chain follows a straight
line as it passes through
the derailleur. If not, con-
sult your bicycle shop.

If the derailleur looks
straight, shift through the
gears to ensure that each

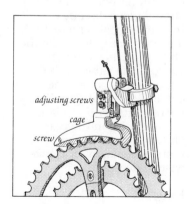

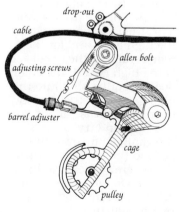

Left, front derailleur. Right, rear derailleur

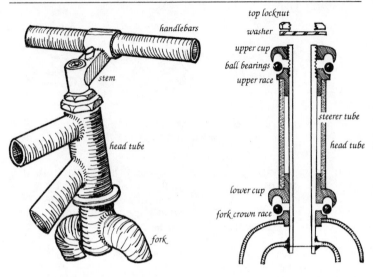

Left , the parts of the steering system. Right, the parts of the headset.

gear works. If you can't seem to find some of your gears, the derailleur should be adjusted. There are two screws on both the front and rear derailleurs. One is labelled H for high gear and the other L for low gear. As you move the shifter, the derailleur moves until it is stopped by one of these screws. For the front derailleur, the large chainring is the high gear, and for the rear derailleur the small cog is the high gear. If the chain does not quite shift into the high gear, turn the H screw counterclockwise about ¼ of a turn and try again. If the chain shifts over and beyond the high hear, turn the H screw clockwise ¼ of a turn. Do the same for the low gear on the front and rear derailleurs.

Nowadays, virtually all new bicycles have index shifters that click into a notch for each gear. To adjust an index system, first adjust the derailleurs as explained above. Now shift the chain into the smallest cog in the rear and the smallest chainring in the front. Click the rear shifter once. The chain should move directly onto the next cog and no further. If it does not quite make the shift, there is too much slack in the cable. If the chain shifts too far, the cable is too tight. Turn the barrel adjuster on the rear derailleur or on the rear shifter counterclockwise to increase tension, or clockwise to decrease it.

Headset

The headset is the bearing assembly that allows you to

turn the front wheel with the handlebars to steer the bike. To check the adjustment, lock the front brake and rock the bicycle back and forth on the ground. If you feel play, the headset is too loose. Hold the front end of the bicycle off the ground with one hand, and point the wheel straight with your other hand and then let it go. It should turn slowly to the side on its own accord. If it does not, or if the wheel has a tendency to stay pointed straight, the headset is too tight.

To adjust the headset, first loosen the locknut with a large adjustable wrench. Then turn the upper cup with a headset wrench. Turn the upper cup about ⅛ of a turn clockwise to tighten the headset or counterclockwise to loosen it. Hold the upper cup in place and tighten the locknut against it. Check the adjustment and repeat if necessary.

As with hubs and bottom brackets, headsets occasionally have to be overhauled. If you are not able to get a good adjustment, take the bicycle to your friends at the bike shop and have them overhaul the headset.

Handlebar Stem

The stem is an adjustable portion of the steering assembly. It can be raised or lowered to attain a comfortable riding position. Handle-

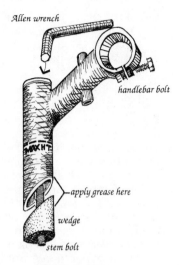

Handlebar stem

bar stems have both minimum and maximum height settings. If you find that you must exceed either one of these adjustments, you should buy another frame size or a different stem.

The only tool required to install or adjust the stem is an Allen wrench. The stem is held tight in the head tube by a binder bolt and a wedge (see illustration). To loosen the stem, turn the Allen head bolt counterclockwise until the stem can turn freely in the head tube. This does not require the loosening of the headset locknut. Sometimes, particularly with chrome-moly frames, rust formed inside the head tube will keep the stem from turning. Try squirting derusting fluid or penetrating oil down into the head tube first. Another method is to strike (not pound) the top of the bolt with a hammer (place a block of wood on top of the stem before you strike it) As part of your regular tuneup, it is a good idea to remove the stem and clean and grease the portion that fits in the frame.

The minimum height setting is dictated by the mechanics of the stem design. If, for example, the stem is placed as far down into the head tube as possible, with the stem neck resting on the headset, stresses placed on the joint could potentially cause the stem to break. If your goal is speed rather than comfort, the top of the handlebar stem should be approximately one inch below the level of the seat. This will give you a more aerodynamic position on the bike, but with increased

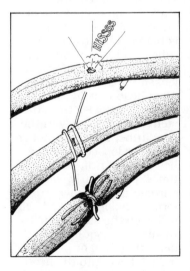

Emergency repair without a patch

stress on your lower back and neck.

Emergency Repairs

In this section you will learn just a few tricks for dealing with the kind of mechanical problem that may occur when traveling. Often, there is no need for despair, and it will be quite possible to make a makeshift repair that at least allows you to get back to civilization.

Flat Tires

Hopefully you will have a spare tube or a patch kit with you if you get a flat tire. There is always the possibility that you'll lose you patch kit and spare tube during your ride or that your tire sidewall blows out. Because mountain bike tires are inflated to relatively low pressures, there are some ways to get enough air into the tire to get you back to civilization.

If the tire is OK and it is just a puncture in the tube, you can usually get by with a piece of string or wire. Remove the tube from the tire and determine where the leak is coming from. Tie the string or wrap the piece of wire around the circumference of the tube at the hole to seal it there.

If you find that your tire case has a hole in it and the tube is hanging out, there are two repair options. The easiest thing is to let enough air out to keep

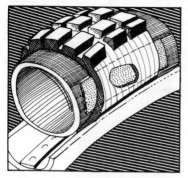

Applying a boot to a damaged tire casing.

the tube inside the tire. There may still be enough air left to keep you from riding on the rim, as long as you don't ride too fast. Another way is to use a tube patch or another piece of flexible solid material placed inside the tire at the location of the hole. Then pump the tire back up.

Broken Spokes

Broken spokes usually occur one at a time, so dealing with them in the boondocks isn't too bad. When a spoke breaks, it almost always causes the rim to go out of true, rubbing against the brake pad. If you disconnect the brake, you will be able to continue riding, albeit a little wobbly and with more caution. Transfer you body weight to help compensate for the loss in braking efficiency.

In some instances, disconnecting the brake won't do the trick, because the wheel hits the frame or the front fork. Tightening adjacent spokes on the same side of

the wheel enough to offset the broken spoke may do the trick. However, you've got to be extremely careful: too much tightening can cause even more spokes to break.

Broken Derailleur

Usually the cause of derailleur problems is a broken cable, but sometimes a crash will break parts of the derailleur itself, making it inoperable. To cure an inoperable front derailleur, disconnect the cable and remove the derailleur from the bike. The body of the derailleur is usually clamped to the frame with one retaining nut and bolt. The only other connection is a small screw at the leading edge of the derailleur cage (see illustration). Removal of this screw allows the chain to be pulled through the derailleur cage. Once the front derailleur has been removed, the chain can be set manually on a chainring, which will allow you to ride back home.

A broken rear derailleur makes life a little more complicated. Make sure you carry a chain tool. You'll often have to remove the derailleur and shorten the chain so the bike can be ridden without the derailleur. To remove the rear derailleur, you will need an Allen wrench. The main body of the derailleur is attached to the rear dropout with one Allen head bolt.

If the derailleur is semi-operable, you can still ride with it. For example, if the main derailleur spring breaks, a piece of wire wrapped around the front and rear portions of the derailleur body (see illustration) will keep the mechanism in one position, allowing the bike to be ridden in one gear. If a return spring for the pulley control arm snaps, a piece of wire can also be used to keep the pulley arm in position.

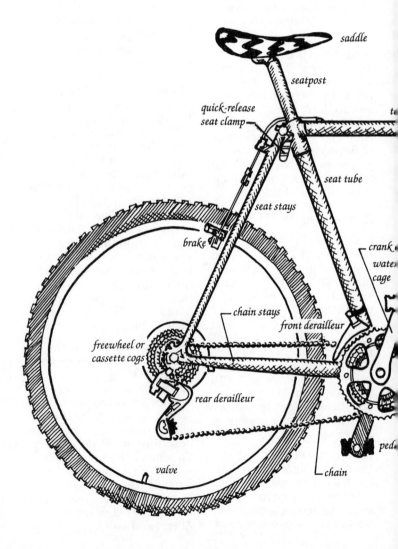

saddle

seatpost

quick-release
seat clamp

seat tube

seat stays

brake

crank

water
cage

chain stays

front derailleur

freewheel or
cassette cogs

rear derailleur

ped

valve

chain

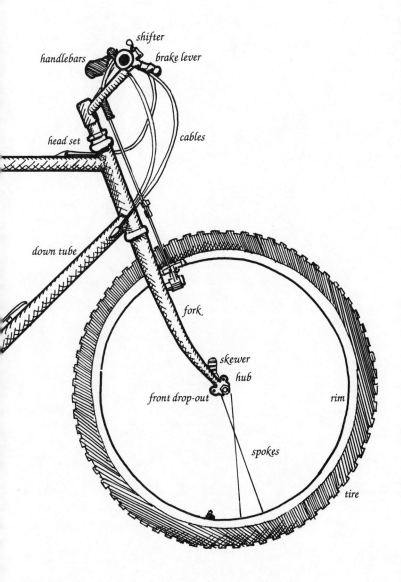

_____ List of Available Titles

Title	US Price
The Mountain Bike Book	$9.95
The Bicycle Repair Book	$8.95
The Bicycle Racing Guide	$10.95
The Bicycle Touring Manual	$10.95
Roadside Bicycle Repairs	$4.95
Major Taylor (hardcover)	$19.95
Bicycling Fuel	$7.95
In High Gear (hardcover)	$21.95
In High Gear (paperback)	$10.95
Mountain Bike Maintenance	$7.95
The Bicycle Fitness Book	$7.95
The Bicycle Commuting Book	$7.95
The New Bike Book	$4.95
Tour of the Forest Bike Race	$9.95
Bicycle Technology	$16.95
Tour de France (hardcover)	$22.95
Tour de France (paperback)	$12.95
Mountain Bike Magic	$14.95
The High Performance Heart	$9.95
Mountain Bike Racing (hardcover)	$22.50
Mountain Bike Maintenance and Repair	$22.50
Cycling Kenya	$12.95
Cycling France	$12.95
Cycling Europe	$12.95

Buy our books at your local book shop or bike store

In the US, book shops can obtain these titles for you from our book trade distributor (National Book Network) or from Ingram or Baker & Taylor. Bike shops can order directly from us. In Canada, we are distributed by Raincoast Book Distribution, in Britain by Chris Lloyd Sales and Marketing Services. If you have difficulty obtaining our books elsewhere, we will be pleased to supply them by mail, but we must add $2.50 postage and handling in the US (as well as California Sales Tax if mailed to a California address) or $4.50 abroad. Prepayment by check, money order or credit card must be included with your order.

North America:
Bicycle Books, Inc
PO Box 2038
Mill Valley CA 94941

Britain & Ireland:
Bicycle Books
463 Ashley Road
Poole, Dorset BH14 0AX